# Worth the Wait

## The Road that Led to Finding True Love

*Thank you for purchasing my book,*

# Patti Turner

ISBN 978-1-63844-881-5 (paperback)
ISBN 978-1-63844-882-2 (digital)

Christian Faith Publishing, Inc.
832 Park Avenue
Meadville, PA 16335
www.christianfaithpublishing.com

Printed in the United States of America

# CONTENTS

# DEDICATION

To Bill Thompson
Thank you for coming into my life so that I might
understand a soul mate and how to love with all my heart.
Thank you for making me promise to write
our story that others may benefit.

To my precious David
Thank you for waiting for me and coming into my life.
You have taught me that true love is worth the wait.
Your love overflows in my life every day,
and you are God's special gift to me.
I love you for eternity.
Faithfully forever yours, my love.

# PREFACE

I believe that the greatest need we have in life is to love and be loved on a deep level by another individual. I believe it is the way God created us because He is the author of love. As stated in Genesis 2:18, "It is not good for man to be alone and God made a suitable helper for him." So what is *true love*? It is love between a man and woman that are truly compatible and connect emotionally, physically, spiritually, intellectually, socially, politically, passionately, etc.—two people so similar that the only difference is one is male, and one is female. Two people raised in different homes yet the same as adults in their beliefs, goals, passions, and love. Two people that love with all their heart, mind, and soul. It is two people that understand the other person's love needs and fulfills that need. They cherish every moment they are together. They bring pure joy to those around because of the love they share with one another. Their love shines like a bright light in a dark place.

I further believe that when we are void of this type of love, it affects people in negative ways that show up physically, emotionally, and spiritually. People will search an entire lifetime for that one true love and settle many times for something less than what truly meets their needs, attempting to satisfy that desire. I have seen people satisfy their need for this type of love by clinging to their children and/or grandchildren and building their life on being involved in their children's lives to the point of smothering them and not allowing them to grow up. I have seen people do this to their pets to the point the pet takes the place of a human being and takes on this roll. This is not fair to the pet, and the pet truly is unable to be an animal for having to be a human to satisfy that need.

This displacement is sad when the person doing this does not realize what they are doing and that the cause is a deep need for love they are not getting. I have seen individuals settle for someone who is totally incompatible or even abusive because they did not believe they would ever find someone or that they are not worthy of this type of love. I have also seen individuals that have settled for someone they felt they could change, only to find out after they are married that we cannot change people.

One of the saddest things I have seen are people who get involved with someone who controls and manipulates them. They end up losing who they are and become a puppet or prisoner to the other person who only wants control and not true love. Those people play on individual's weakness and emotional needs and make it difficult to get free. I have seen a lot of damage done that can take years to heal from this type of relationship. I have seen Christians marry with the only thing they had in common was their faith. Just because two people are Christians, it does not mean they are to be together. Marrying the wrong person can literally be *hell on earth*. I believe people settle for the wrong person because they do not understand their own love needs or how to find the person that meets those needs.

We often recognize true love when we see it but do not know how to achieve it for ourselves. Have you ever observed two people together, and they were so into each other that they were unaware of those around them? You could see the way they looked at each other and could see the chemistry between them. They would be holding hands or sitting closely next to each other. You could see the joy and happiness on their faces because they were with each other and enjoyed the life they shared together. Do we wonder why we see so little of this type of love in our world? Why is the younger generation so disillusioned with the very idea of marriage?

I believe it is because we have failed miserably in finding true love that lasts forever and stands the test of time. In all honestly, we were not taught by our parents, society or churches how to find this type love or what it looks like. Why have we accomplished so much in the world but failed in the one thing that we truly need? Is it no wonder the family is breaking down? We must correct this now before it is too late, and this must start with us taking responsibility to correct it in our own relationships and showing the next generation the way.

My experience and qualifications to be able to speak about this comes from many years of observing adults in different relationships—good and bad. I personally have failed and succeeded in different relationships myself. I watch people interact with their partners on a regular basis and can often tell what type of relationship they have by the way they interact, facial expressions, and body language. The happiest and most joyful people I have ever known are those who have found their one true love and live in a loving relationship every day.

If I had a magic wand, it would be my desire to give this type of love to every person I meet. Since I do not have such a wand, it has been my passion and purpose in life to share what I believe to be true in the steps to finding this true love and keeping it alive every day. I will attempt in this book to give you guidelines, practical steps in finding this type of love, and paint a picture of what this type of love looks like.

I will share my own failures and successes in my road that led to finding true love.

The most important advice I can give anyone is that you must want this type of love bad enough to not settle for anything less and wait till that one person comes into your life who is right for you no matter how long it takes because trust me when I say it will be *Worth the Wait.* If you have settled and are with the wrong person, you must be honest with yourself and acknowledge this. Then be willing to let God lead you to the type of love he created you to have. This may be hard, but nothing worth having is ever easy. Life is too short to live without love and happiness. We serve a loving and forgiving God that is always there to forgive and lead us in the right direction, just for the asking.

Patti Upchurch, Daniel, Puckett, Thompson, Turner
(All the different last names qualify me to write this book as you will soon read.)

# CHAPTER 1

─── ✌ ───

# Marrying Too Young

As children, growing up we learn how to love by the example shown by our parents. If our parents had a loving relationship in their own marriage, then we learn how to find love in a mate by that example. If our parents did not have a healthy loving relationship, then often we grow up searching for something more out of a desire to have something better. Unfortunately, we seek to find that type of love in ways that do not work or by trial and error because we have no guidelines to go by. The clear steps to finding that one true love is not laid out for us; and therefore, we are doomed to fail, not really knowing what to look for or how to find it. Only a burning desire to find true love that last forever exists.

I personally grew up with a mother that had a difficult childhood. She lost her father at a young age and was left with a mother to raise her and seven siblings as a single mom during the Great Depression. For many reasons, my mother was unable to show love or express affection, so the only love I felt as a child was from my father and paternal grandmother. Luckily for me, they were both very loving and affectionate caretakers, so I always knew and felt they loved me. But once again, a loving relationship in a marriage situation was never demonstrated to me. I was a loving individual and had always wanted to be married and give my heart completely to one man.

When we are young, we are immature and do not have the wisdom to make the right decisions that impact us for the rest of our lives. We often make decisions by our feelings and emotions at the time, never evaluating things on a mature level. That was the case for me when I was dating a guy my senior year in high school and felt I knew what true love was. We had a few things in common, but at that age, I did not understand the importance of compatibility or being aligned on a spiritual level. I also did not understand how to love or even what my emotional needs were.

Most people at this age are not equipped to assess if they have the same interests, likes or goals you are both working towards accomplishing in life. This is because at a young age, we are still trying to figure this out yourselves. We have miserably failed on a social level (and as a church body) to educate our children in finding true love and a mate for life. All they know is what is seen on television and movies, which paints a horrible picture of love. Their idea of a mate may be wrapped up in lust, desire, and sex and may not even include love.

Society suggests we try people out like buying an outfit. If the dress does not feel good or fit, take it back and swap it for another item. Sex has become totally void of love and emotion and has become recreational. It is no wonder we have so many emotionally divided individuals in the world. They are void of the one thing they need the most: to love and be loved on a deep level. This affects every part of our being and who we are as individuals. It affects how we interact and perceive other people. Sexual abuse and misconduct are at an all-time high in recent years because of this.

One year after I was out of high school at the young age of nineteen, I decided to marry my "true love." He was twenty-one years old and less mature than I was. I believe now that the age limit for getting married should be raised to a more mature level where you can utterly understand what you are doing and what making a commitment for life means. It was clear a few months into our marriage the differences we had on so many levels. Spiritually, we were worlds apart. I had become a new Christian and was growing in my faith every day. He wanted no part of Christianity or church and even forbid me to go to church. I had to hide and go to church on Sundays while he worked on the weekends with his job.

As I grew spiritually, we grew apart. He did not want me to be a Christian because he said it changed me, which it did for the better. There is a definite reason the Bible tells us to not be yoked together with unbelievers.

> For what do righteousness and wickedness have in common. (2 Corinthians 6:14)

On our first-year anniversary, we had a huge argument, and it was clear things were not going well in our marriage. A couple of months later and a few more heated arguments, I came home from work one day to find a note on the kitchen table from him. To summarize he said, "I have left you, and the next time you hear from me will be with divorce paperwork for you to sign."

My hopes and dreams of love for a lifetime came to a screeching halt. (Keep in mind this was before the days of email or smartphones, so I had no way to reach him to try and work things out.) A few weeks later while at work, I was served with divorce papers including the date and time to appear in an attorney's office. When that time came, I

wondered what I would or could do to change my situation.
I walked in the attorney's office to see my husband sitting
there, and my only question was, "What has happened to
us?"

He said, "You have changed. We no longer have anything in common, and I want a divorce." He went on to say
that right before we got married, he realized it was not going
to work, but he did not have the heart to tell me when we
had the entire wedding planned.

I responded with, "It would have been better to tell me
then because it would have been easier to not marry me THAN
to marry me and then divorce me!" I calmed down and later
asked the attorney if I had any options.

He said, "Your husband is filing the divorce on the
grounds of irreconcilable differences, and even if you con-
tested it, the state cannot make him live with you."

So with a broken heart and spirit on that sad day, I
signed the paperwork to end a marriage that had not even
survived two years. I remember reading in my Bible in 1
Corinthians 7:15:

> But if the unbeliever leaves, let it be
> so. The brother or sister is not bound in
> such circumstances; God has called us to
> live in peace.

Lesson One learned: Do not get married too young!
You just are not mature enough to understand what you are
doing and even what compatibility means. Enjoy your single
life, date, and find out the difference in people and what you
are looking for. You can only find this in dating different
people, and when it does not work out in a relationship, you
learn from this and take it as the next lesson in life. When

you have finally learned what works and what you need, then you may be ready to find that one true love but not before.

Over my lifetime I have seen too many people get married too young, only to end up divorced. I am not saying all are that way, and I do know some high school sweethearts that have made it. But I also know some that have stayed together for too many years for the sake of the children, even when they and the kids would be much happier to divorce. There are many reasons for people to try and make it work in marriages and relationships, but as my own daughters have stated to me from first-hand experience, children are not one of them. If you do feel you made the mistake of marrying too young, then it is not too late for you. As I state later in this book: There is true love for everyone.

Patti and her sister on her wedding day

# CHAPTER 2

## Staying Married for the Sake of the Children

Many times, we meet someone, fall in love, and think that because we have something major in common, this is enough to hold a relationship together for a lifetime. There may be a lot still missing in the relationship, but we feel the one passion we share is strong enough to hold the relationship together forever. This was true for my second marriage. I was determined if I married again, it would be to someone who I could connect with on a spiritual level, and this would be enough to hold the marriage together.

At the age of twenty-four years old, I felt I had again figured out true love and all it entailed. Never was any one person ever so wrong about any one thing as me. When I met my husband, there was no physical attraction. We did not have any of the same hobbies or similar backgrounds. The only thing we did have in common was we were both Christians and felt we had a calling on our lives to be in ministry. At the time, this seemed to be enough to make a marriage work for a lifetime.

I was a very romantic person, loving romantic music, candlelit dinners, moonlight walks, holding hands, cuddling, and physical touch with someone. Having read the book, *The Five Love Languages: The Secret to Love That Lasts*, by Gary Chapman, I realize now that my primary love languages are physical touch and words of affirmation. If I had known the importance of that then, I would have made sure the next person I married had those love languages or could communicate with me through those love languages. Again, this was as far from the truth as could be possible when I entered my second marriage. I knew on my wedding night what a horrible mistake I had made. My thought at the time was I made a commitment to my husband and God, and I prayed somehow things would get better.

Immediately after we were married, we both enrolled in a Christian college to prepare for the ministry. Focusing on a purpose and a direction for our lives kept us distracted with all that was lacking in the relationship. We made friends with other couples, and it seemed as if everyone had their own struggles, so maybe that is the way marriage and life were supposed to be. Words like "I love you" were occasionally said or written in an anniversary card with no true deep feeling. At times, I felt so much was missing in our relationship only to reassure myself by thinking, *It is supposed to be this way when you are married. You are not supposed to be starry-eyed in love. You are not supposed to be romantic or passionate in your relationship. You are just supposed to be a wife that is submissive to her husband and take care of his needs.* I always thought by staying in the marriage, it would bring me great rewards in eternity, and at the time, if I could just learn to be content in all situations, I could be happy.

Four years into our marriage, we graduated from a Christian college and were both licensed as ministers. We went straight into our first church for my husband to pastor, and I would assist him. We took up the life of pastoring churches, which was rewarding but also stressful. Finances were tough because pastors make extraordinarily little money. We lived in homes provided for us, which were not always the best. As the church denomination appointed us, we moved every few years to new churches in different areas.

Our first daughter was born four years into our marriage. It seemed by having a child, this would bond us together, and we would be closer. Children take up time, and you find after they are born, you have less time to devote to your relationship just for the sheer nature of time involved in raising a child. Relationships, no matter the status of children or your life, must be a priority that both people see importance of making time for each other. This was not the case in our relationship.

I will pause here in my story to give an example of a couple I know of that has chosen to make their child the supreme priority and what it has done to their relationship. This couple married and a few years into their marriage, had a little girl. When the little girl was around six years of age, she developed a love for gymnastics. The little girl was an amazing gymnast, so the parents wanted to provide her the best possible training. The town they lived in did not provide the best, but a larger town four hours away did. The husband had a great job in the town they lived in, so they could not afford for him to leave his job.

The couple decided the mother and daughter would move to where the training was available four hours away, and the father would come visit a couple of weekends out of the month. This went on for several years. The father visited less and less because he got tired of the long drive on weekends. This couple clearly did not make their relationship a priority in their family or lives. I will stop here and say to some, it may seem I am judging, but I am not. I am merely proposing when we prioritize our relationships, the other parts of our lives will benefit. When we do not, our relationships will most likely fail.

We must demonstrate to the next generation what a loving relationship looks like. Deciding to be apart from your spouse when you do not have to be is telling a child the relationship in a marriage is not important. This can potentially result in your child making similar mistakes when they are grown because they have seen the examples of children coming before the relationship. We are living in a loveless society, crying out to find true love that lasts a lifetime. We owe it to the next generation to show them what this love looks like. This will only happen when we make the decision to make our relationship with our mate a priority over all other costs.

The greatest sense of security we can give a child is to be a part of a family where the husband and wife put their relationship first and then demonstrate their love to the child. That child will, in turn as an adult, seek to find a mate where the same example holds true for them. I personally have spoken to many children and adults who had parents demonstrating this type of love. All of them agreed on how secure they felt in their family relationship. They knew the love between their mom and dad was strong and felt nothing could possibly destroy it. It gifted them to seek out that type of love as adults.

Turning back to my story: Eleven years into our marriage, a second daughter was born. She had come as a blessing after previously having a miscarriage and losing a child. Again, moving from church to church and pastoring were always a struggle financially and also on the family and children always changing schools, friends, and homes. After a series of events, my husband had decided he would do overseas missions, and I would raise the children and work full time, and he would go forth overseas several times a year to do mission work. This allowed him to stay in the ministry and offered stability to the children to stay in one home and make friends. So several times a year, he would be gone weeks at a time overseas doing mission work, and I would remain at home, taking care of the children and working.

Absence does not make the heart grow fonder when the relationship is already on rocky footing. Over the years, my husband had begun to show signs of mental illness and demonstrated traits of paranoia, schizophrenia, and narcissism. Following the appearance of these symptoms, we had attempted to go to several different Christian counselors to work on our marriage. Each counselor recognized the signs of mental illness as I listed, but my husband did not. In one on one counseling sessions with them, they would tell me that because of his condition, he would not recognize his mental illness or the need to seek treatment. They all advised me to leave and divorce him. My response to them was I cannot do that because God had not given me a reason to leave him.

I would just pray every day that God would somehow provide a miracle, and all would be right one day. The one thing I did not realize over the years was how this was impacting my daughters and the example it set for them of what a marriage looks like. I also did not realize I had essentially imprisoned myself by staying. I was never allowed to be true to myself. I had to be what my husband wanted me to be. I was not allowed to speak and think my own thoughts. I had to conform to his needs, and I became totally void in my own personality, not realizing my own needs or desires were never taken into consideration, and everything of myself was sacrificed for someone else. It was a very empty feeling. I dealt with it by lying to myself that all was well in my marriage and family. Trust me when I say that you can make yourself believe almost anything if you tell yourself this enough. This can be an amazing mental tool if used wisely but can also be detrimental when it is abused as I did.

I have always felt close to my daughters because I felt I was the main parent in their lives and spent so much time with them growing up. Their father was away a lot, and it gave me time to make wonderful memories with them. As my older daughter went through her teenage years, I could see the need she had for acceptance and love from her father, which was not there. Much later in life, I realized that if daughters do not receive this from their fathers, they often gravitate to the wrong men who will control and manipulate them for their own gain.

I am sad to say that was the direction my oldest daughter went when she met a young man at the age of seventeen. He was extremely controlling and manipulating to the point he convinced her to leave home at age eighteen and marry him. And for over two years, we had no contact with her. Shortly after they were married, she became pregnant. And after the baby was born, he became abusive. Luckily, she was smart enough to get the baby and leave him one day. She called me to come get her so she could get away from him.

Unfortunately, her life would never be the same. Several years passed, and he took my granddaughter and convinced his daughter to have nothing to do with us. This is an example of the repercussions of staying in a toxic relationship. It is so important to either be single or in the right loving relationship to be able to demonstrate this to your children. It can have a ripple effect on your children and then your grandchildren and even great-grandchildren. We must stop this somewhere and make it right for the next generations to come.

What happened to my oldest daughter had a profound impact on my youngest daughter and our marriage. I always wondered if there was something I could have done different and what went wrong when this terrible turn of events unfolded. My husband continued to go back and forth overseas, staying gone weeks at a time while I remained at home working and taking care of our younger daughter. He had returned after one of these mission trips and was sick and went to bed early.

Before I retired to bed, I went to shut the computer down and glanced up at an email he had been working on. I kept seeing the words, "my wife," "my wife" and wondered what he could be writing someone about me. After twenty-five years of marriage to this man, I was not prepared for what I would read next. He was expressing his undying love to a woman he had met overseas and telling her he was looking for a new wife, and she fit the profile and asked her if she was interested in him. I was dumbfounded. Never in my wildest dreams would I have ever thought my husband would have been unfaithful in any way to me.

Of course, I have described in twenty-five years, we did not have the best of marriage, but never had I ever been unfaithful or entertained the thought that my husband in the ministry would be unfaithful to me. I printed out the email as evidence of what I found and went to wake my husband. I asked him what the email was about and when, if ever, he had planned on telling me these facts. His response was he was going to tell me in a few weeks. He said he did not love me and did not want to be married to me anymore.

I asked him, "Where in your Bible does it say you can divorce your wife because you decide not to love her anymore or do not want to be married to her anymore?" Since he was a minister after all, he should know the answer to this question. But he had no answer because there is no place in the Bible that states this.

That night before I went to sleep, I fell on my knees by my bed and prayed and asked God why He had not heard my prayers to heal my marriage. I had prayed that prayer every night for twenty-five years, and I had prayers answered many times in my Christian life. Why not this one?

In a still small voice, I heard God speak to me and say, *I heard your prayer each night, and I have answered that prayer.* It was then that I realized that God, knowing me so well, knew I would never leave that terrible marriage I was in, so He removed me from it so I would someday know and feel real true love. So after twenty-five years in a terrible marriage, my husband, who was mentally ill, divorced me, allowing me to be free to finally find true love. At the time, I did not realize why this happened to me, and it would be several years later when I least expected it that I would understand this.

Pastoral Couple (Patti and her second husband)

Patti with her daughters (Maria age eight and Felicia age one)

# CHAPTER 3

# Single Adult Life

I suddenly found myself single at the age of fifty. It was terrifying. Not only did I have to figure out how to be single again after twenty-five years of marriage, but I also had to figure out how to continue to provide for my family who depended on me. I was now alone with an older adult daughter, a granddaughter, and my youngest daughter living with me. To make matters more difficult, my father also needed care since he had recently been diagnosed with Alzheimer's.

My home had been severely neglected for many years because of my ex-husband's absence and him not wanting to take care of it. It was the first and only time since the age of fifteen that I was not working. A couple of years prior to this time, I had stopped working to help care for my infant granddaughter and help with my father's care. The financial burden to care for all my loved ones seemed insurmountable. What type of job could I possibly get that would allow me to work out of my home so I could continue to take care of the family members that needed me and still make money?

Within a noticeably short time, God provided just the right job to provide for all my financial needs. God provides for our needs when we turn it over to Him and trust Him! I was able to get all the needed repairs done on the house, pay the bills, provide for my family, and take care of my loved ones all at the same time. I then decided to attend a divorce care program at a local church. It was a six-week program aimed to guide you through the different stages of divorce, help you through your emotional recovery of the breakup of your marriage, and place you on the road to healing. These types of divorce care programs also provide courses for the children of divorcees as well.

I have learned over the years that you can only give your heart to someone else once you have allowed yourself enough time to recover emotionally from a previous relationship and are completely healed. DivorceCare recommends you remain out of any serious relationship for one year for every four years of marriage. For me, that would have been six and a half years, and I personally think it depends on the individual. However, you should wait until you are emotionally healed before moving on.

I feel everyone is different, and there is no set rule. Healing from divorce is not easy. It is a long, sometimes painful, process. I have seen individuals rush right into another marriage or relationship, and for several of my friends, it ended in disaster. An example of this is a dear friend of mine who was feeling very lonely and inescapably rushed into another marriage too soon. He had met a woman and dated her for a few months before he rushed down the aisle. He was far from being emotionally healed from his recent divorce. It was difficult to be at the wedding and watch him make a terrible mistake. He was only married a few months before it ended. Years afterward, he was still paying for this mistake financially and emotionally. The lesson here is if you go through a divorce, you must allow yourself time to heal.

Following the divorce care program, I found a single adult class in my church to get involved with. We had Bible studies, social outings, ministry opportunities, and built strong friendships within the group. I found other divorced ladies like myself who I could do activities with like walking and going out to eat. My new single life was beginning to take on a purpose and meaning. I finally had time to self-examine and work on ways I could improve myself. I think we always need to be examining ourselves for ways we can improve. I do not feel we ever arrive to perfection but always striving to be a better person. If we have selfish tendencies, we can work on being less selfish and learn ways to lift others up.

I would find myself looking for ways to make someone's day better again—saying an encouraging word or doing a special deed. This helps yourself more than it helps the other person. I opened my home up to single adult Bible studies and cookouts. I suddenly realized how much single adults are all alone, and they are often outcasted even in church communities. The divorced person is suddenly labeled a damaged piece of goods, and churches often frown upon this group. They are the most neglected group of people in the church today. I was part of a large church, and they did not even allow us to mention in the church bulletin that we had a class for single adults, even though this class was the hardest working group in the church and the most dedicated.

At Thanksgiving when families are all gathered in a home for a meal, single adults with no families find themselves alone at home. My first Thanksgiving single, I found myself all alone crying and eating a can of soup while my children were with their father's family. I told God then that I would do whatever it took to make sure no one ever had to spend Thanksgiving alone again. Every year after that, my single adult class spent Thanksgiving at my house eating a big meal and then crowded around the television to watch sports or a movie. I went to great lengths to make sure no one I knew that was single spent Thanksgiving alone again.

We had become one big family. If someone needed something, we found a way to help. Once a month, we had a "Take Care of Each Other Day" in which we would go and work on a single person's home for whatever they needed or if someone was sick, we took meals or helped in whatever way we could. This is exactly what a family does. Divorced people are often isolated from their families and have no one to care or look out for them. If every church would see the great need here and realize the opportunity for ministry, then we could provide a place for so many divorced people to belong and feel at home.

Let me also stop here to say Christians are the only army to shoot their wounded. What I mean by this is, we in the church are the first to judge someone for being divorced. Often assuming the person did something wrong to make this happen. God calls us not to judge but to love people.

> Do not judge, or you too will be judged. For in the same way you judge others, you will be judged, and with the measure you use, it will be measured to you. (Matthew 7:1–2)

Having gone through a divorce myself, I am very compassionate to divorced people, and having worked with single adults for many years, I had an opportunity to minister to many individuals. The overwhelming need I found for these people were to be accepted and loved for who they are at that time. Anything that needs to change in their lives will be taken care of in time by God. It is not our calling or purpose in life to change people. It is our purpose to love people and accept them right where they are in life. No one gets married with the thought of being divorced one day. If they did, then they would not have married. It just happens to people for a wide range of reasons.

My desire is to guide people into the right relationships where they find love that lasts a lifetime so they never have to experience divorce. It is way too painful to go through; you want to avoid it if you can. I choose to use my pain to help others through their divorce and to find purpose in life again. My hope is they can learn from past mistakes, find purpose again, and use this to move on to a better life for themselves.

I will stop here to address the issue I have found among so many Christians about remarrying once you are divorced. Let me qualify and say that I graduated from a Christian college with a bachelor's degree that included a minor in Bible. I have studied and restudied the New Testament and all the passages that address divorce and remarriage. I have studied the Greek translation and examined every word. This is something you must do yourself and come to your own understanding and have a peace about. I will only give you my thoughts on this subject.

I serve a loving God that if we confess our sins, he is faithful and just to forgive us of our sins. I have been a Christian since my late teens and walked with the Lord a long time. The loving God we serve does not hold one decision or mistake against us. When we repent, he allows us to move on with our life. He does not ask us to suffer for that mistake until we die and not find the love he created us to find.

God wants only the best for us, and if we missed his best, he still wants us to find it. If my search for true love had ended after my divorce, I would not have found it and would not be writing this book today. It is because I believe this so strongly and God has placed this truth within me that I am writing how to find this love now. If you have closed yourself up in a box and think, *I cannot come out and find love because*

*I made a mistake*, I trust and pray you will listen to me and have the courage to see a different truth. The best is yet to come. Believe it; it can happen to you if you do not give up and you wait for God's best. It will be worth the wait! Trust me.

Now back to the lesson. The next issue is for those who are in a bad marriage or relationship and see no way out of it. Once again, I am not advocating divorce or encouraging couples to split up. I am writing my story to encourage others to make the best decisions about their relationships. I will tell you in my lifetime, I have seen many couples who are obstructive to one another, stay married to each other for decades or life. They are not happy and are in fact miserable! They stay together for the sake of the children or because they made a commitment and feel they must honor it. Trust me, I understand because for twenty-five years, that is exactly what I did. But I realized in time, it was damaging for my daughters and for me.

In retrospect, I do not feel that was the right thing to do. If I had had the courage to leave, my daughters would have been so much better off, and I would not have wasted twenty-five years of my life that I can never get back. That is a lot of time to waste and exactly why I would like to prevent others from making the same mistake. I meet people all the time that are older and say, "I am too old to start over."

I personally know of a couple who have been married thirty-eight years. It was a marriage of two people that married young and had truly little in common. They were unequally yoked spiritually and total opposites politically as well. They stayed together for the sake of their three children. Eighteen years into the marriage, they decided to sleep in separate bedrooms. The wife told the husband she did not want to have sex with him anymore, so for twenty years, they have lived together in the same house as roommates. They take separate vacations and talk little. I recently was around the man, and he was one of the unhappiest people I have ever known. This is not a marriage but a prison. No one will ever convince me God approves of this or commands you to stay in this situation.

I know of another couple that have been married over thirty years, and they sleep in separate bedrooms because one of them snores. Let me tell you in this day and time with modern medicine, sleep studies, and CPAP machines, there is no reason for couples to sleep in separate bedrooms due to snoring. And in case you think I do not know about this, my husband and I sleep together with CPAP machines. Nothing is going to keep me from sleeping in another room away from the man that owns my heart. I cherish the closeness we share as we sleep together in each other's arms. This is the way it is meant to be.

One of the most intimate times between two people is when they are sleeping side by side, touching each other, and feeling the very pulse and heartbeat of the other person. This contributes to a couple's bond that cannot be denied and grows over time. Do we love our mate enough that nothing will keep us apart? If this does not hold true, then we may not be with the right person, and it is time to examine what needs to be done to make this right. I do not care how young or old you are; life is way too short to spend any amount of time with the wrong person. God does not want us to live this way.

I know of another couple married over thirty years. The man met a woman while in his early twenties. He fell in love with her and wanted to marry her. He felt this woman was truly his soul mate. They lived on opposite sides of the country, and the woman was not willing to relocate. She obviously did not feel the same way as the man or nothing would have kept her away from him, even distance. She broke up with him, and they never married. His whole life, even into his sixties and after marrying someone else and having children, he still thinks constantly about the woman he lost that was his soul mate. Could it possibly be he married on rebound or is his wife not the right person that meets his love needs? It is sad that someone would spend an entire life grieving the loss of someone they loved.

As you will see in the next chapters, I understand the loss of a soul mate, but you must find a way to put this behind you and move on. Life is way too short not to be in a loving relationship that meets all your needs.

Patti single again at age 50

# CHAPTER 4

—— ❧ ——

# A True Love Story (It Could Be Yours)

This is my once upon a time love story. It begins, of course, with two emotionally available adults—a single woman and a single man. The single man had been without someone in his life for several years after being in a terrible marriage that should have never been. The single man believed deep down in his heart one day he would find his soul mate. He honestly believed there was a woman he would one day fall in love with and connect on a soul level.

He was a true romantic that believed in romantic music, romantic movies, slow dances, holding hands, and waiting to kiss that special lady until it truly meant an expression of your love and affection. He believed when this happen, it would be a slow kiss that you would feel in your heart. He was willing to wait for such a lady. Knowing he could never make this happen on his own but in the right timing, it would happen when he least expected it.

In the meantime, he would be content living his life alone and urging others to seek and find love. He would tell everyone that crossed his path that *love* was the most important thing in life. It was the glue that held the world together and made the world a wonderful place to live. He was not one to go on a date with someone just to have a date but chose to wait until he felt the date meant something. It needed to be with someone whom he genuinely wanted to be with. So dating would be saved for the special someone that would come into his life, and he would be willing to wait and not settle for anything less.

On a side note, I understand it is rare for people to experience the type of love written about in this story you are about to read. It is my hope that as you read about our love, it inspires you to not settle for anything less than the type of love described here. Now back to the love story.

Now the single woman had come out of a failed marriage as well. A marriage between two people that had little in common and never connected on a soul level. However, she never lost her passion and was a true romantic that enjoyed romantic music, romantic movies, slow dances, long walks, starlit nights, holding hands, and long slow kisses that truly meant something deep down in your heart. She believed in loving with all your heart, holding nothing back when you found your soul mate.

She believed good things come to those that wait and knew not to settle for anything less than the best life has to offer you. She knew you could obtain this if you are willing to wait. She believed there was a man like her that existed who would be her soul mate, and in the right time, he would come into her life. In the meantime, she would enjoy her life fully. Her free time was spent enjoying the best life had to offer and appreciating every moment of every day.

Both the single man and woman understood life is a gift to be cherished and not taken for granted. She spent time outdoors listening to romantic music, dancing (which was her true love), and meeting new people to inspire and encourage along life's way. The woman and her friends went to a weekly singles dance where they would meet new people and dance the night away. It was a wonderful event—dancing and seeing her friends enjoying themselves. This single lady loved people and was not shy, so it was not uncommon for her to ask a man to dance. "Just to dance" with no expectations only to enjoy herself. Little did she know that this would be the venue that would allow her to meet her soul mate. Her greatest enjoyment in life was dancing, so how natural it would be to meet someone that had the same love of dancing because soul mates connect on all levels?

One such night at the singles dance, this single lady saw an attractive, well-built, nicely dressed man sitting at a table and went over and asked him to dance. He accepted, and they began to dance. This dance was different than any other dance she had ever had with anyone. She asked him his name. It was at that moment she knew only his name, but deep down in her soul, she suddenly knew she had everything in common with this man. The more they talked about the things they liked and disliked, the more this proved to be true.

They both loved music and dancing and were true romantics in every part of their being. They liked the same foods, movies, hobbies, and were the same age but never looked it. They felt like teenagers at a high school dance and suddenly felt young again. It was like looking in the mirror, but it was another person. Could it really be possible to find someone so like yourself in every way? They danced the rest of the night together, enjoying each other's company and the sheer pleasure of dancing. How exciting and fun that night was!

At the end of the night, the man told the lady he would like to meet her the next week at the dance. She agreed. He mentioned since they just met, it would not be respectful to ask her for her telephone number, so he would not. The following week and for weeks to come, they met at the dance. They danced, talked, and got to know each other. They both liked freestyle dancing, and they moved on the dance floor as one. People would stop, turn, and look at two people so moving in sync with one another; it was amazing to watch. They never knew anyone was looking at them because they were in their own world on cloud nine. He looked at her as if she was the only woman on the face of the earth, and she looked back at him as if no other man had ever existed. You see, that is what they had waited their entire lives for. They could look at each other and see down into their very souls.

A few weeks later, the man asked the lady for her phone number. He thought about her constantly and wanted to hear her voice during the week. They lived a far distance apart, and both worked so they were only able to see each other on weekends. They would wake in the mornings and talk to each other on the telephone first thing, and as soon as they got off work, they were on the phone again. There was great pleasure in listening to the voice of the other person. Such anticipation came for weekends when they would finally see each other for the long-awaited dance together.

Several weeks later, it came the Friday night of the lady's birthday. She wore a beautiful red dress with red high heels, and to the man, this was his "Lady in Red." He asked the DJ to play this song, and they danced a long slow dance to the ballad. This would become their song, and every time it was played at the dance, everyone who had seen them together knew this was their song. All eyes would be on them to watch them dance together in their own little world singing this love song to each other.

The next night would be their first date. They would go out with family and friends to eat and dance to celebrate her birthday. For her birthday, the man would give her a beautiful princess fairy angel that reminded him of her elegance and grace. She was his special angel. They both loved collecting angels and strangely enough had no two alike. That night a friend drove, and on the way back home, they were in the back seat of the car listening to romantic music playing. Just talking and enjoying being with each other. Talking came so easy for them since they had everything in common. They loved being together and cherished each moment. It was at this moment that the man leaned over and gently kissed the lady.

It was a long slow kiss that reached down to their very hearts and gave them butterflies. Neither persons had each ever felt this way before with anyone and knew this was incredibly special. The kiss truly meant something special and was so magical that it made the moon and stars shine brighter. People kiss each other with no meaning or feeling, but this was totally different. They both felt this kiss deep down in their souls, and it felt as if their hearts would burst open. At this moment in time, they knew they never wanted to be apart.

As weeks went on, they continued to meet at the dance each Friday night and saw each other on weekends. During the week, they could not wait to hear each other's voices on the phone. One weekend while together, the man turned to the lady and opened his heart fully and expressed how much he was in love with her. Holding nothing back, he would love with all his heart and give all his heart and soul to this lady. She turned to him and expressed the same to him holding nothing back and with no fears or barriers. For you see, when you find your true soul mate, you know you can trust them with your heart, and there is no fear.

Never had two people been so open with their hearts completely to each other. They had waited a lifetime to find each other and love, so there was no holding back. Each night they would write a love letter expressing how they felt and mail it to each other. A love letter would arrive each day in their mailbox. What the mailman must have thought delivering letters with hearts drawn all over the envelopes and scented is funny to imagine! They were truly in love and wanted to shout it from the rooftops.

When in the car together, they would stop along the side of the road, play a romantic song, and get out and dance under the moonlight. Two hopeless romantics seeking a venue to express their love. When they were together, they were holding hands, and when they went out to eat, they had to sit next to each other so that they could be close and touch the one they loved. They would wait in a restaurant no matter how long it took to have a table they could sit next to each other. It brought many smiles to waitresses and hostesses to explain why they could not sit apart because they were two souls intertwined.

Months later, they were together on a Christmas Eve exchanging gifts. They had carefully chosen gifts they knew the other person would enjoy. The lady had bought her man a leather coat that she knew he would look so good in and enjoy. The man bought his lady diamond earrings that he knew she would love. He saved one last present to the end, and when she opened it, she saw a diamond engagement ring. The man dropped to his knees and asked his soul mate to marry him. She embraced him. She knew they were meant to be together from the beginning of time and said yes. What a joyous Christmas, planning their lives together knowing there would be a time they would never be apart.

They planned for a church wedding in the springtime. Time for either of them could not go by fast enough. They took long walks holding hands, stopping along the way to kiss, and planning their future. They continued to meet each week at the dance because that is what they loved. The people at the dance found out they were to be married and told them they were an inspiration for others. The man would keep his job when they were married and make the long drive each day to work—a small sacrifice to be with the one you love and have waited your entire life for.

It came that beautiful spring day for their wedding. They were to be married in a small white church with family and friends present. Her daughters would be her attendants, and her granddaughter the flower girl. His best friend would be his best man; he had lived next door to him for many years. The music was carefully planned out by the lady to express the true love they shared. The lady would wear white at the request of the man. To him, she was his angel and the only woman for him. The man would wear a handsome black tuxedo.

As the service began and the music played, the man patiently awaited his bride. The attendants came down the aisle, and then came the time for his bride to come in. He beheld the most beautiful woman in all the world to him and could not believe she would soon be his wife. A lifetime of waiting for this very moment. His princess angel was soon to be his, the lady of all his dreams. She saw standing there the most gorgeous man she had ever laid eyes on, and he was the love of her life, her soul mate. Never were two people more meant to be together, and everyone present on that day could attest to that fact. They stood before the minister, family, and friends, pledging their love and commitment to each other. After exchanging rings to symbolize the unending circle of their love, there came a pause in the service and as a surprise to everyone the bride sang the words to the song "When God Made You" by New Song to her groom:

> It's always been a mystery
> to me how two hearts can come
> together and love can last forever.

Now that I have found you
I believe that a miracle has come
when God sends a perfect one.
Now gone are all my questions
about why, and I've never been
so sure of anything in my life.

Oh, I wonder what God was
thinking when he created you.
I wonder if he knew everything
I would need, because he made
all my dreams come true.
When God made you, He must
have been thinking about me.

I promise that wherever you
may go, wherever life may lead you,
with all my heart I'll be there too.
And from this moment
on, I want you to know I'll let
nothing come between us.
And I will love the ones you love.
Now gone are all my questions
about why, and I've never been
so sure of anything in my life.

I wonder what God was
thinking when he created you.
I wonder if he knew everything
I would need, because he made
all my dreams come true.
When God made you, He must
have been thinking about me.

He made the sun, he made the
moon to harmonize in perfect tune.
One can't move without the
other, they just have to be together.
And that is why I know it's true,
you're for me and I'm for you.
'Cause my world just can't be
right without you in my life.

I wonder what God was
thinking when he created you.
I wonder if he knew everything
I would need, because he made
all my dreams come true.
He must have heard every
prayer I've been praying.
He knew everything I would need.
When God made you, I thank
God he made you, yes he did.
When dreams came true,
you are my love, my life.
When God made you,
he must've been thinking.
About me.

The minister pronounced the man and lady as husband
and wife, and he kissed his bride. With smiles on their faces
demonstrating the happiness they felt at that moment, they
walked down the aisle as husband and wife. After a beautiful
reception, they drove to an elegant hotel next to the airport
where they would spend a wedding night that would set off
fireworks. The newlyweds awoke the next morning and flew
to Maui for a two-week honeymoon.

Upon arriving in Maui, they drove to the place they would spend their honeymoon—a beautiful three-bedroom home on six acres of private land overlooking the ocean with a private swimming pool. As magical as their meeting and courting were, the same would be true of their honeymoon. When two truly romantic souls come together, romance is felt in everything you do from cooking a meal together and then stopping to feed each other bites of food to grocery shopping and sneaking kisses in the aisles. From cleaning house and chasing each other with the broom or vacuum, only to giving in to being caught because you know what will follow. From taking baths and showers together for the sheer pressure of bathing each other's bodies so that you can fully appreciate and enjoy every inch of the person that owns your heart. You cherish every second of every day and never take a moment for granted. For this is true love to the deepest level; it never changes or ends but lasts for eternity.

Their honeymoon was filled with swimming naked in the pool to making love under the stars with the sound of the ocean waves applauding their union. When they made love, it was slow and lasting but with all the passion of two lovers long waiting for each other, desiring to love and please each other in every way possible, giving all their body, soul, and spirit to each other. Two bodies merging together as one soul that finally found where they belonged: with each other. Never had either of them felt so loved and complete. It was as the world stood still to allow them to fully enjoy each other's love.

They took long walks along the ocean, went on romantic sunset boat rides, long drives in the mountains, stopping along the way to enjoy the beauty and take a long-lasting embrace and kiss. Each night they fail asleep in each other's arms as that is where they belonged and soon found they could sleep no other way. The most restful and heavenly sleep each of them had every felt, totally engulfed in the arms of the one you love. They were meant to be together and always felt incomplete without the other one next to them day or night. Soul mates are like this!

Each morning they awoke to tell each other how in love they were and eager to express that love. If they awoke during the night, they took the opportunity to express their love for each other. They had long breakfasts, enjoying the new day and joy of being together. Evening meals were candlelit dinners with romantic music, gazing into each other's eyes, holding hands while eating. There is great pleasure in the simple touch of someone you are so in love with and connected with. It makes you long for the moment you can touch again when you are apart.

Long passionate kisses make you look forward to the next embrace and cherish the ones you have had. Romantic music and slow dances together were a common occurrence. The lady loved singing love songs to the man of her dreams and took every opportunity no matter where they were to do so. It was as the world stood still to enjoy these simple but special times. Did the rest of the world feel these things? Do other people find their soul mates, and does everyone find true love as they had?

After returning from a blissful honeymoon, they would begin a life together that was very much a continuation of their honeymoon. Days were spent getting up and going off to work while eagerly awaiting coming home to spend each moment possible with each other. They desired to be together every minute because they had waited their entire lives to find each other. They functioned as one now and found it more difficult to be apart. When they were together, they shared everything: cooking, cleaning, eating, shopping, exercising, walks, showers, sleeping, EVERYTHING.

It was not an obsession as you might think. It was loving someone so much that you cannot bear to be apart even for a moment. You find sheer pleasure in sharing everything together. It is thinking about the other person more than you think about yourself. When you are out places and see something you think that person would like or enjoy, you get it if possible. Being with your soul mate is leaving little "love notes" for them to let them know how your heart overflows with love. It is thinking of ways to express your love and making the other person happy in any way you can. Always putting the other person's needs and wants above yours.

Eight months into this beautiful union of two souls, there would come a day like no other that would shake their world to the very core. It would be the day that the man was diagnosed with a terminal disease that would take his life. He was only given a few months left to live. How could it be that two people wait a lifetime for each other to only enjoy one another for a couple of years? Oh, how life has its awful twists and turns!

The man informed his doctor that he wanted to be kept as comfortable as possible and spend his last days at home with his wife. In the end, the lady that had become his soul mate took off work to care for him and be by his side every step of the way. This was truly where she belonged—to walk with him from this life to the next. For she knew once he was gone that one day, they would have an eternity together to dance for he was created for her, and she was created for him. When the awful day came of his passing, the lady was holding the hand of the man who owned her heart, loving him with all her very being as he passed from this life into eternity.

You might say it would have been better if they had never met than to have found each other after waiting their entire lives and then lose the other person. They both agreed in the end that they would not have regrets about not finding each other sooner. For it was worth the time they did have than not to have had the time at all.

The moral of this story is do not settle or hold back. For if you are willing to wait, your soul mate or true love will come. And if you love with all your heart, you can experience a lifetime of true love even if it is for a moment in time.

Patti and Bill wedding picture

45

Lady in Red (Patti)

# CHAPTER 5

—— ❧ ——

# My Journey in Grieving My Soul Mate

When my husband passed away, to say my world was totally shattered is an understatement! I found myself for the first time in my life completely numb and abandoned by God. I know now that God had not abandoned me, but the overwhelming amount of grief I felt at the time kept me from feeling anything. I forced myself to get up every day and function only because of the routine I created and followed like a robot—doing things and tasks I had to do with no thought or feeling. No one could help me through this process because grief is an individual response and emotion a person must sort through themselves.

I was extremely fortunate that my daughters and friends gave me the time and space to work through this until I could function again as a somewhat normal human being. What I did not realize was that I would never go back to be the person I once was before all this happened. I would have to create and develop the person I was all over again, and this is a process that I would like to share for the benefit of others that may find themselves in this place.

From the moment my husband and I were married and bonded together as soul mates, we shared everything together, from sleeping, bathing, eating, cooking, cleaning, shopping, leisure time—everything—but working, and that was only because we had separate jobs. What I felt, he felt. We could complete each other's thoughts and sentences because we even had the same thoughts. This is the true nature of soul mates. So when my husband was diagnosed with cancer, we shared the pain of his disease as well.

During his dying process, I was with him every step of the way. I felt his pain. I cared for him twenty-four hours a day and rarely left his side except for brief moments to take care of necessities. This bonded us even closer together in the end. I was holding his hand and loving him deeply when he took his last breath. It was at this moment I was thrown into a shock and existence I had never known possible. For days, weeks, and even months, I was numb with no feelings at all. I felt totally lost and unable to function in the simplest of tasks because everything I had done prior to this was with my soul mate who was no longer there.

I could not understand what was wrong with me. I went from feeling wholly engulfed in the love of my soul mate to a state of emptiness and loneliness I never knew existed. Many people, even my children, tried to reach out to me, but no one could help me. I would reach for an outstretched loving embrace only to feel empty as nothing could satisfy my deepest need. I could not sleep or eat, and weight loss became my enemy. I tried to swallow food only to have it come back up and force it down again.

My medical doctor put me on liquid supplements to keep me alive for the first six months of my husband's passing. Because my functioning ability meshed into another human being, I became disabled to continue to live once he was gone. When he was ripped apart from me, it was like splitting a molecule. I had to learn how to function alone again instead of two fused together as one. It felt impossible to do anything without my soul mate, and no one knew what I was going through to help me.

People suffer loss in their lives—broken relationships, death of a relative, mother, father, child or even a spouse. The loss of a soul mate is different, and I soon discovered after his passing no one in my circle of friends or family had ever encountered this. I found myself aimlessly walking around looking to fill a void that could never be filled. I was constantly at a loss for words. I felt like a wayward animal seeking shelter but never finding it. No one knew what was wrong with me to help, and I did not know how anyone could help me either. It was a hopeless feeling that at the time seemed to never end or bring relief. I longed to be normal again and function in the world like everyone else but somehow knew it was not possible. So what did I do? I wandered around for two years in a maze, searching for an opening to life again before I found the answer. What I experienced in those two years searching I would like to share as a warning to those going down this path feeling grief.

Soul mates are very loving people that give and receive love freely to one another. They can express this love easily and comfortably. When you have had this type of relationship and are suddenly left without your soul mate, you find yourself desperately craving that love and warmth. You will respond to the resemblance of this even when it is not genuine because of your deep desire to find your place again in life. Because of this, my recommendation to you is to make some close same-sex friends to do things and share with. Avoid romantic relationships with the opposite sex until your healing is complete. This is true after any type of breakup. You need time to heal alone. Beware of persons of the opposite sex wanting to console you because they care or feel bad for you in the condition you are in.

After the death of a soul mate, you will find yourself pulling away from family and close friends. This is because you are unsure of your true feelings about anything in life, so for fear of hurting someone, you limit your interaction with your loved ones. Please know it takes time to work through this to get back to where you once were or to find yourself in a different space. Ask those who love you to try and understand and support you in this time until you work through the healing process.

After I went through counseling, grief support groups, and did much reading on the grieving process, my liberating moment came from discovering a book entitled *Grieving a Soulmate* by Robert Orfali. He described his journey of losing his soul mate (his wife) and the grieving process as well as the recovery. He states:

> One of the big challenges for grieving soulmates is how to disentangle the interlocked identities. As a soulmate, your identity is totally fused with that of your partner's. It's the nature of soulmate love. We tend to complete each other's thoughts. We feel our pain together. When one hurts, the other hurts. We share a common history. Our separate egos have fully bonded and we are one. Instead of being two separate "I's," soulmates fuse into an entity called "we." Instead of two single atoms, soulmates become a single molecule. This explains why soulmates can experience total, non-egotistical, and unconditional love.

So what happens when death does us part? The answer is: The surviving soulmate becomes an "I" again—a single atom. A big part of your healing process centers on re-balancing your identity. You must become whole again, which means you'll have to re-create your identity without the physical presence of your loved one.

Finally! I found someone that understood what I was feeling and going through. This was a freeing moment for me in my pain and grief. I now knew the way to become a whole person again. I began to learn how I could recreate myself. But I would have to find out how to do that in absence of my soul mate. When my soul mate died, he took everything that matters in my life with him. This explains the total devastation I felt after his passing. My soul mate was the one person in my world who could have helped me through the grieving process if he had not died. He would have been the one to give me a shoulder to cry on, help me when I was trembling in fear, and aid me in finding life again.

The loss of a soul mate generates the deepest type of grief a person can experience. This type of loss is completely different from the loss of a parent, child or even a spouse who is not a soul mate. This is because soul mates are perfectly intertwined and fused together. This is the nature of their bond and why they are soul mates. Because of these facts, grieving a soul mate must be a solo act, which means solitary, unmitigated, and big time grief. Therefore, grieving a soul mate becomes complicated grief. It is a situation where the grief does not resolve itself with the passing of time. The survivor simply withdraws from the world and barely functions.

Life has no meaning and left unresolved can wreck a person's life with serious depression.

Symptoms of complicated grief include anger and bitterness over the death, recurrent pangs of painful emotions, distressing intrusive thoughts related to the death. This is no fun and very painful. Many grief therapists believe that we must break all ties with our dead soul mate to be whole again, which is the end-goal of the grieving process. The problem with this theory is that it does not work for soul mates. You cannot break the bond between soul mates. You must find how to be whole again with their physical absence gone while recognizing and accepting they will always be a part of you. The idea that we love our soul mates in absentia.

With this theory, we can see the part they have in our lives while they are physically absent but at the same time benefit from their comforting presence in our hearts and grow stronger in this knowledge. Our memories of them go from being a source of pain to a source of strength. It is coming to the realization that you have only lost the physical presence of your soul mate in your life, but they still live inside of you and are very real there. They are always kept alive in you by the memories you have of them. What a natural place for them to be and a safe place for you to hold them and move ahead in wholeness with your life.

Because of the place they hold in your heart and life, does this mean you are never ever to love or be in another loving relationship? Absolutely not because you recognize what you have is unique and can never be replaced with anyone else. This allows you to heal and love again but in a different capacity. You would never want anything to take the place or take away from your soul mate, and rightfully so, it should not. This special bond cannot be broken, which is why it is so unique. This will always be special between you and your soul mate and something you can cherish knowing they will always be a part of you. But healing in this will allow you to open your heart to love again in a different capacity and never take away from what you hold inside of you. It means you can think of the memories and times with your soul mate in a pleasant way and know how special it was for you. It is placed in a safe and special place in your heart and mind. There is no trying not to think about these memories but allowing them to come and bring you strength and healing, recognizing the significance they have in your healing as well as in your life.

You do not have to talk about your soul mate to others in remembering this, but it is a special bond between you and your soul mate. I found myself feeling free to talk to my soul mate without thinking there was something wrong with me. It was a natural act, and I recognized this. Each day I found myself becoming more of a whole person and recreating who I was. I became a person who lost a soul mate whose presence was very much still a part of my life but functioning in his physical absence.

It is my desire that anyone who has lost a soul mate to first and foremost know that this is a unique grieving experience. You are not crazy but unique. May you find wholeness in your journey while still holding on to the special place your soul mate has in your life. Cherish this and know how blessed you are in having had that person in your life. Your strength will come from the love you shared with them and knowing that you are free to love again.

I found the words to the song "Immortality" by the Bee Gees to express my emotions during this time:

> So this is who I am, and this is all I
>     know.
> And I must choose to live for all that I
>     can give,
> The spark that makes the power grow.

And I will stand for my dream if I can
Symbol of my faith in who I am.
But you are my only, and I will follow
    on the road that lies ahead.
And I won't let my heart control my
    head.
But you are my only.

We don't say goodbye, we don't say
    goodbye.
And I know what I've got to be
Immortality.
I make my journey through eternity.
I keep the memory of you and me,
    inside.

Fulfill your destiny, is there within the
    child.
My storm will never end.
My fate is on the wind, the king of
    hearts, the joker's wild.
We don't say goodbye, we don't say
    goodbye.
I'll make them all remember me.

'Cause I have found a dream that must
    come true.
Every ounce of me must see it through.
You are my only.
I'm sorry I don't have a role for love to
    play.
Hand over my heart, I'll find my way.
I will make them give to me.
Immortality.

There is a vision and a fire in me.
I keep the memory of you and me,
    inside.
We don't say goodbye, we don't say
    goodbye.
With all my love for you, and what else
    we may do, we don't say goodbye.

Patti returns to dancing with the help of friends

# CHAPTER 6

‿∾‿

# Finding True Love for Eternity

The world has taught us through loss and disappointments that holding back part of your heart in a relationship is the safest way to live. Sometimes we feel it is best to leave a part of our self to go back to, acting like insurance before we are hurt and disappointed by someone else. What if they are not what you wanted or needed or they were not able to give themselves completely to you? This is called going into protection mode.

The problem with this mode is it keeps us from experiencing the type of love where you give your all to someone, and they give their all to you. The love where you can trust with your entire heart because they will love you with every part of their being till death you do part—two hearts coming together and beating as one, needing the very air that the other one breathes. Never imaging a day without the other and rejoicing in every moment they have together in celebration of their love. The type of love that covers all and loves through all of life's hardships.

This is not a fairy tale love because I know it exists and have had the privilege to experience this type of love twice in my life. I know it is possible for those who choose to seek this type of love and never settle for anything less. May my next love story inspire you to find this type of love in your life and keep it!

\*\*\*\*\*

Once upon a time, there was a man that lived his whole life in search of his one true love. He was determined not to settle for anything less than the woman who was the perfect fit for him, like him in every way possible, and a woman he could trust to give his entire heart, body, and soul to. He wanted someone who would love him in the exact same way he would love her. For him, it was better to live a fulfilling single adult life than to settle for anything less than his Cinderella. So much of this life was spent trying to find his true love and in wasting time in disappointing relationships, only to discover they were not the one he was looking for. These women would claim to love him, but over time, they only proved their insincerity. There came a day when he would say to God, *I cannot find her on my own. I turn this totally over to you.*

There was a woman who had experienced many disappointments and losses in her life only to find herself alone again after the passing of her husband. She had so much love to give. She could hardly imagine living the rest of her life alone. She loved with all her being, giving her heart and soul completely, and was looking for the one man that would love her in the same way. So many people want that type of love but do not have the ability to reciprocate the same devotion. She had met men over the years wanting to love her in this way for them to only prove they would not give all their heart to her. These men proved to never really understand her type of love.

She knew she could never settle for anything less because it was the only way she could love. As painful as it was, it would have been better to be alone the rest of her life than settle for a man who could not love her back in this way. Could there be a man left in the world who had the ability to love in such a way? She had found her soul mate and this type of love before, but she wanted to experience love in a different way. A man she could love with all of her being that was perfect for her in every way and someone looking to love her in the same way. There came a day when she would say to God, *I cannot find him on my own. I turn this totally over to you.* Little did she know but would later find out that was the same day a man was praying the exact same plea.

Two weeks after this monumental day, the woman was on a singles website and came across a profile of a man that was close in age to her and lived close by. Upon closer examination, she saw he went to church of the same denomination as her. Could he possibly go to her church? She decided to send him a message and see. Very shortly after sending the message, the man responded stating he did go to the same church and would like to speak with her. They initially talked on the phone to get to know each other better. The more they talked, the more evident it became that the two were alike in so many ways: close in age, same likes and dislikes, the same personalities, and most of all, seeking the same type of love that each of them agreed was most difficult to find.

The day would come that they would meet and go on their first date. It would be one week prior to Christmas. When her doorbell rang, she opened the door to the man that would change the rest of her life and be the answer to her many prayers. The moment she met him, she felt something in her heart connect with him. He was so much like her in every possible way. Could it be possible to find the love she was looking for?

Their first date was magical in every way. They would go to a Mexican restaurant for an opportunity to share a meal and a lifetime of experiences that brought them to this place. So many heartaches and disappointments paved the road that led them to each other. But for that night, all those letdowns seemed nonexistent. They could only see the eyes and heart of each other and the strong connection between them. There was a mariachi band playing at their table as they smiled and shared the warmth of the music with their hearts playing the same tune. Could this be the love the man had waited his entire lifetime for knowing someday he would find it?

Not wanting the evening to end, they decided to drive in search for Christmas lights. There was a college nearby that always put up a large display of Christmas lights, and they chose to drive through and see what they could find. As they drove through the beautiful sparkling color of luminescence, it was obvious there were lights glowing within each of their hearts too. The man politely asked if he could kiss his special lady, and it was as if their lips melted together. Where had each of them been their entire lives, and why did it take so long to find each other? Questions that would never be answered on this side of heaven, but for this moment in time, it felt very much like heaven to them. As the man took his special lady home, they knew deep down inside this was not the end of a night but a beginning of a love story they would create and build upon each day for the rest of their lives.

As they began to date, it was evident it would take longer for the man to realize this was real than the lady. He had been misled so many times in previous relationships. It took him some extra time to trust the sincerity of the lady. She was patient to wait because she knew from the first evening she met him that he was the long-awaited answer to her prayers.

As Valentine's Day approached, he invited her to go away with him for a few days to a special place where he had lived earlier in his life, Charleston, South Carolina. He had been a disc jockey on a local radio station there and spent several years in this beautiful city. He wanted to share his favorite town with her. His best friend was also there, so it was an opportunity for the lady to meet him as well. Little did the lady know she would fall in love with Charleston, and it would soon become her heart's desire to live in this beautiful southern town.

They planned the trip, and when they arrived in this romantic city by the ocean, he surprised her with a beautiful hotel room right on the beach at the Isle of Palms. There were days filled with sightseeing of the historic city and nights filled with gorgeous sunsets and the sounds of the ocean lulling them to sleep. It would be here in this romantic setting that the man would express his love to his long-awaited lady. It was the start of many days ahead where the words, "I love you," would be said between them throughout the day. Their hearts were so full of love they could not hold back expressing it; the love just comes out. They had to be touching each other all the time for the closeness of their soul yearns for it. It was the making of two hearts and lives being meshed as one and an eternal bonding.

So many people do not understand this type of love they were experiencing. It was a mystery to some how two people can love in this way and allow their hearts to be completely open for someone to hold and carry forever. As months of their beautiful love story unfolded, they planned another special trip to the serene island of Kauai that May. The special lady needed to go for business and invited her man to accompany her. He had never been to Hawaii, and it was a special place she was excited to share with him.

Kauai is an island that has magnificent sunsets, unbelievable colored rainbows, and scenery that must resemble what the Garden of Eden looked like. Everything there is lush and green with spectacular mountain ranges, bluer than blue oceans, and romantic white sand beaches. It was such a special place for the lady to take the one she loves and share with him all of God's beauty. They would sit on the lanai (porch) of their condo and watch the sunrise each morning. They would watch the ocean waves come in and take sunset sailboat cruises. Then would come the day they would hike the long treacherous Na Pali Coast Trail.

This would prove to both of them that they will always be there for each other no matter what comes their way in life. This winding treacherous trail in a mountainous rainforest allowed them to see how they would always have each other's back and look out for each other no matter what came in their lives. They decided then they would face life together.

When you share the love they shared, you always look out for the other person because they own your heart, and you can never imagine a day without them in it. You cherish just the little things like holding hands, sharing a sunrise or sunset together or being amazed by a rainbow in the sky. The man and lady would share the same love of God's beautiful creation and nature, and what a perfect place it was to share these feelings. It would be in this special place on their last night on the island of Kauai they would go to a beautiful hotel for cocktails to watch the last sunset.

With the spectacular colors of the horizon shining through, the man would turn to his special lady and ask her to marry him. Of course, her answer was yes because she had waited a lifetime for him, and the moment would soon arrive they would seal this with a kiss forever and ever. It was a night of celebration afterward telling everyone around them what just happened. It was a night forever ingrained in both their memories.

Months following the couple's engagement were spent planning a wedding for September. Because the man worked second shift and his lady worked first shift and they lived in different cities, they were only able to spend weekends together. Being apart only made them long for the time they were together and cherish every moment. They would always make it a point to talk on the phone each day and send messages of love to each other. Their love grew more and more with each passing day. Planning to combine two households into one can be challenging for some people, but for this couple, it was long-awaited anticipation that was the challenge. The wedding could not come fast enough. So it was decided that she would move into his house and the process began.

The morning of their wedding day started with a beautiful sunrise as if creation were celebrating the union of two lost lovers finally coming together. The bride arrived at the church with her sister and prepared herself in a wedding dress she had picked with her bridegroom in mind. She was not nervous but thrilled at the possibility of finally sealing their love and commitment before family and friends—a day she only hoped and dreamed would happen with a lover so genuine and perfect for her.

The groom was nervous since at fifty-nine years of age, he was getting married for the first time. He had waited a lifetime for his special lady who would own his heart and give herself so completely to him. The lady heard individuals make comments about her man saying older people who have never been married are "spoiled goods," and that is usually the reason they are still alone at this age. She ignored them all as never was this farther from the truth than in this case. The lady soon found out how much she would be loved and adored by a man who finally waited for just the right one to come along and take his last name. (Oh, how we so cut ourselves short when we close our mind to certain possibilities!)

So as the music played, his bride walked down the aisle and stood by her daughters and the groom's best friend by his side. They would say their vows and profess their love before family and friends to start their new life together as one. What a wonderful wedding and reception they had. They felt not only the support of family and friends but most importantly, the approval of the Lord who had brought them together. A beautiful honeymoon followed, filled with passionate love making where love radiated through each other's bodies. It was the expression of the purest form of love to give their bodies to each other in this way. It allowed them to give all their love to one another and receive all their love on a soul level. It was a spellbinding beginning to their marriage.

People who marry often think they could never love the person beside them any more than the day they were married. But true love grows more with every passing day. As you wake each day beside the one that owns your heart, you are full of excitement because they are there to share the day with you. Every moment is savored. Showers together become a welcome pleasure when shared with someone you are so in love with. You find yourselves always wanting to touch and connect with the person who has become so much a part of you. As you grow to know everything about your spouse, you fall deeper in love, and unconditional love takes on a whole new meaning.

Are people perfect? Absolutely not! But love covers small impurities when you are perfectly matched together, have so much in common, and love on such a deep level. You find yourselves protecting that love at all costs because it is so pure, and you would never jeopardize losing it. Again, so many people do not know how to love on this level, and if they start down this road and try to find it, they often mess it up by focusing on the impurities. Love truly can cover a multitude of sins when you are not focused on all their coarseness and love with a forgiving heart. True love must be protected and nurtured always.

The first few months of their marriage was amazingly easy in so many ways. There seem to be no adjustment for the man or woman as they started their lives together. It was effortless just like they were always meant to be together, a perfect fit in every way, loving life together day by day and appreciating every moment they had with one another.

As the years went by, the man and lady loved each other deeper with each new day and continued to plan out their life together. They would often take trips back to Charleston, South Carolina, and each time, the lady would pray they would someday live in this great southern town and move out of Atlanta, Georgia, where they both were from. The day came when the man was offered early retirement and asked his lady where she wanted to retire. Charleston, South Carolina. What a quick answer it was! The only place she had ever wanted to live since she found it.

They planned to sell their home and move to Charleston. But so many things had to happen first to make this dream come true. They had to sell their home for just the right price since homes were more expensive in Charleston, and the lady had to quickly find a job to replace her current one. They committed all their plans to the Lord knowing that if God opened the door, he would make a way. They worked hard to finish improvements on their home and prayed about the right realtor that would list the house for the right price. One was found, and he agreed to list the house higher than the market value and wait and see what happens.

Within twenty-four hours of the house going on the market, the house had three contracts higher than the asking price and a bidding war took place! They were able to close on the house with more than they dreamed possible they would get. They soon made a trip to Charleston, and the first job interview the lady went to, they offered her the job for the money she needed. Another miracle had occurred, and everything was falling into place. Moving day came, and with the help of family and friends, they packed up all they owned in two trucks and drove to Charleston to start their new life.

Many people at that age range would never consider moving that far away from family and friends to start all over again, but that is how dreams become reality. You must commit your dreams to the Lord and allow Him to direct your paths, and he will make your way straight.

Upon their arrival, God provided a small condo on the water with beautiful sunrises for them to live in until they could find their dream home. They had certain requirements: a main living area on one floor, a quiet neighborhood location, and beautiful nature to look through a screened-in porch to sit and enjoy it. God would soon provide such a house, and within two months of moving to Charleston, they would move into their dream home together. Days would be spent enjoying their piece of paradise and appreciating all God had done for them but never forgetting how things were before they found each other.

Life was so much more fulfilling now for them, and simple things like sitting beside each other, holding hands, and talking became the highlight of their day. The lady loved cooking and taking care of the man that owned her heart and loved her in a way she never knew was possible. He made her feel like a special princess every day, and loving him more and more is all she ever wanted to do. In her heart, she knew she had found the perfect man for her—the man God created just for her. Their love was so perfect and effortless. They never took a day for granted but loved each other as if it were their last day together, always looking for new ways to express their love and see it grow stronger.

She knew that there could never ever be another one in her life because she never wanted to love anyone the way she loved him. She prayed when their time came to pass from this world into heaven, they would go together like in her favorite movie, *The Notebook*. But if that was not the way God chose for it to be, she never wanted anyone else in her life. He was perfect for her in every way, and because she had God's best, she was simply too satisfied with what he had already given her. Their love was meant to be for eternity, and that was the way it would be. She would always be his forever faithfully!

The words of this Journey song entitled "Loved by You" expressed her true feelings in finding her "True Love for Eternity":

> Every time is like the first time tenderly
> Loving you is like breathing spring
> Seasons change but your heart beats
>     constantly
> Count my blessings every day as you love
>     me
> As the sunset disappears across the north-
>     ern sky
> You look for forever in my eyes
>
> All I can say, long as I have a voice
> I'll thank God above that I was your first
>     choice
> If I should die before I wake
> I'll go into the night whispering your name
> If lying in your arms is the last thing that
>     I do
> At least I know that I'll be loved by you
>
> In about a hundred years from now
> When all my love letters are found
> And someone reads these words I've writ-
>     ten only meant for you

They'll know how forever came true
If I should die before I wake
I'll go into the night whispering your name
If lying in your arms is the last thing that
    I do
At least I know that I've been loved by you

So let the years roll on by
These are the best times of my life
I'll just smile when my days are through
Knowing that I've been loved by you
At least I know that I've been loved by you

Patti and David wedding day

Patti and David on closing day of their house in Charleston

# CHAPTER 7

— ✦ —

# Guidelines to Finding Your "One True Love"

In this chapter, I have provided some guidelines for you to follow while you are on your journey of finding your "one true love." I have seen success in these with myself and others. To start, if you are looking for a long-term commitment that leads to marriage, you can only date people who are compatible with you and have all the qualities you are looking for in a mate. Do not waste valuable time in dating someone that is not going to go the distance for you. When you do not make this a prerequisite, valuable time is wasted and keeps you from finding your "one true love."

These relationships where two people have everything in common and know how to love each other are the ones that last forever. When seeking to find the right person, you must make a commitment to be focused on the ultimate outcome and stay the course to make it happen. Never settle for anything less but the one person that is right for you and meets your love needs. If you are willing to commit to this purpose and not settle, it will be worth the wait, no matter how long it takes. Remember, love is not always defined by number of years but by quality of time spent with the one you genuinely love. Now let us begin.

1. *Work on yourself.* What I mean by this is you must be the best version of yourself you can be before you can give yourself to someone else. You must be willing to give your all to someone and not take. Over the years, I have worked with a lot of broken single adults, individuals who have found themselves in terrible unhealthy relationships. And it left them damaged and insecure in so many ways. They often found themselves broken, lonely, and very needy for love and attention.

   Human beings in this state starving for love and affection come across as very needy, even if they are trying to hide it. In order to avoid this, we must heal from past relationships and move on to a healthy state before we can freely give love again and open our hearts up to be loved. When you are a needy person, you are not in a good position to find someone. If you are in this unhealthy state, you need to spend some time self-examining and be open and honest with the things about yourself, which might need changing. Too many times, we often want to rush into another relationship before we have given ourselves enough time to recover and heal from the previous one.

   There are a couple of great programs I have participated in which have helped me and my friends to become whole again. One I highly recommend is called DivorceCare. It is a twelve-week recovery program that guides you through the process of healing from a divorce. Here you will find support from others that have experienced what you are going through, and those who lead the group have been there, found healing, and understand you. They even have a program for children of parents going through a divorce. This type of program helped me so much. I went through it twice and then became a leader to help others.

Another program I found helpful for those who have experienced a loss of a loved one is GriefShare. It is a thirteen-week program that walks you step by step through the grieving process and recovery. Again, you will find support and help in healing from the pain of losing a loved one. I cannot stress enough the importance of healing from broken relationships before moving on again. You truly must be ready before seeking another person in your life. If you are not sure, then you probably are not ready yet. So many individuals rush into another relationship without recovering from the past one. DO NOT MAKE THIS MISTAKE. Take the time to heal and love yourself first.

If these do not apply to you and you feel you are by this time ready to find your "one true love," then a great guideline is to ask yourself if you possess these qualities found in 1 Corinthians 13:4–8:

Love is patient, love is kind. It does not envy, it does not boast, it is not proud. It does not dishonor others, it is not self-seeking, it is not easily angered, it keeps no records of wrongs. Love does not delight in evil but rejoices with the truth. It always protects, always trusts, always hopes, always perseveres. Love never fails.

I feel one of the biggest obstacles today in people finding their "one true love" is they do not know how to love themselves. We must feel good about who we are before we can give love to someone else. God is the author of love and the creator of love, and I am constantly looking to Him to show me how to love not only myself but others. When I feel good about myself, I feel free to love someone else. You must work on this long enough to feel confident in this. There can be many factors over a lifetime creeping into our lives and causing us to not feel good about who we are. Therefore, you must work on these things first. No one wants a person to bring their baggage into a relationship. It can be damaging to a romance. Seek God's help for direction. Learn to forgive yourself and others who have hurt you.

You must come to a place where you are comfortable being alone. Only when you do not need someone to become whole are you then ready to receive someone in your life. What I mean by this is you do not have to have another person around to enjoy life. I have met so many single adults who tell me they cannot stand to be alone. If you are at this place in your life, you must ask God to help you be content in all circumstances no matter if you are alone or in a relationship.

When we are so desperate to have someone else around, we will settle for the first person that comes along just so we do not have to be alone. This is a recipe for an unhealthy and ultimately unhappy relationship and life. As Paul wrote in Philippians 4:12, "I have learned the secret of being content in any and every situation." If you struggle with loneliness, find a single adult group that you can be involved with to make friends and do activities. This is a great way to bond with others like yourself on the same walk of life while working to love yourself. It is only once you have completed these steps that you are ready to find your "one true love."

2. *Find your love needs*. We must know what we need in love before we can find someone to fulfil that need. It sounds simple, but believe it or not, most people do not know what they need in love. They just want someone they are attracted to and someone to love them and maybe someone they have a few things in common with. That is a recipe for disaster and relationship failure.

I personally was in my fifties before I understood my love needs, and it was not until I read the book, *The Five Love Languages*, by Gary Chapman that I understood the differences in individual's love needs. I thought love was all the same and everyone showed and received love all the same. This book shows how this is not true. Being with someone who does not understand your love needs can make you feel very unloved no matter how hard the person is trying to show their love for you.

We need to understand the love language of the person we are with and how they receive love. And we need to be able to communicate to the one we are with how we feel loved. The five love languages as outlined in the book are physical touch, words of affirmation, quality time spent with someone, acts of service, and gift giving. After I read this book and learned the importance of knowing and understanding love languages, I made sure my children, friends, and family had copies. Many single adults have shared their reasons for filing divorce. The most common reason was miscommunication of love. How can we receive love if someone does not understand how we feel loved? How can we show love to someone unless we know how they feel loved?

When I was single and started dating someone, one of the first questions I would ask if they had read this book. If their answer was no, then I gave them a copy to read and let them know if they were serious about dating me, they needed to read the book. I would give them a specific deadline to read it, and we would talk about their love language and mine. I needed to know they understood this profoundly serious point in a relationship. Everything else builds on knowing how to love and be loved. Now you do not have to follow my strict actions here; however, it is extremely important to understand how you receive and feel love and how your partner feels and receives love.

3. *Learn to give love.* True love is where every part of your being is in love with the person you find to be the only one for you. It comes with a strong desire to give love for the sheer pleasure of loving the person who owns your heart. You give expecting nothing in return. Your heart knows what your mind has confirmed that the person you are in love with is perfect for you in every way. You trust them to own your heart because you are assured they feel the same love for you, and they are right for you in every way possible.

You find yourself thinking of this person in the past, present, and the future. You cherish every moment you have together for the mere pleasure of loving them. You find when you are with them, you have a need to be close to them and touch them because you are becoming one in body and soul. You find the desire to share everything with that person because of the pleasure of being with them.

When you really understand this type of love, you will not be able to settle for anyone less than the one who will reciprocate this type of love in return to you. It is not loving to get love. It is loving for the sheer pleasure of demonstrating your feelings for another person. You think of them every day, long to be with them, and would never do anything to diminish the love you share. You nurture it every day, and it grows more and more with each new day.

You love this person in such a way that you do not see all the little flaws they have, but instead, you appreciate all the things about them that made you fall in love. Loving someone in this way is exactly what Paul was talking about in 1 Corinthians 13 when he describes love as patient, kind, not being proud, not dishonoring, not self-seeking, not easily angered, not keeping a record of wrongs, always protecting, trusting, and never failing. When we truly can love someone in this way, we have the loving relationship God created us to have.

4. *Find someone you have everything in common.* One of the secrets to finding your true love is finding someone like you that you have a lot in common. I have often heard the term, "opposites attract." From my experience in observing relationships, that is

the farthest from the truth. Observing this philosophy is like waiting for an explosion to happen.

When two different people come together with different opinions, this will eventually lead to an explosion. I have a personal example of this. I once worked with a girl who demonstrated my point here very well. My co-worker and her husband were total opposites. She told me they rarely agreed on anything and were constantly rubbing each other the wrong way. She said over the years it had become a game in which they would try to do something vindictive and hurtful to the other one to "outdo" what had been previously done. When I asked her if she enjoyed being married like this, she told me "No, I can't stand him."

I then asked, "Why do you stay in the marriage?"

And her response was, "For the sake of the children." What a terrible example for those children. Opposites may initially attract, but after years of disagreement, they will repel.

There is pure joy and happiness in a relationship where two people have things in common. You enjoy sharing the same things in life: dreams, recreation, political views, spiritual views, food, sports, economic status, philosophy on raising children, etc. The list goes on and on. I have had people ask me over the years about individuals they were dating, and they would tell me, "We have a couple of things the same we like, but he likes sports and I do not", or "He likes certain type music, and I like another type. He likes to do different things than I do on his days off."

All I can think is how do they think this will play out long term? I will tell you because I have witnessed it. They will start to spend less and less time together and spend more of their time with family and/or friends that like the same things they like to do. The couple will not grow closer but apart.

Let me also state how important it is to date and marry someone who is exactly where you are spiritually. So many marriages have been lost over this one issue alone, and too many people have stayed in marriages waiting for the one who does not believe to come around only to waste many valuable and unhappy years. People make decisions to commit their hearts to God when they are good and ready, and you cannot make this decision for them. Our faith is so important to us as individuals that it is essential we are aligned on this.

It is important to find someone that you like everything about, who is as close to you as possible. We should never try to change anyone to make ourselves happy, and we never want anyone to try and change us for this reason. What happens is people wind up compromising themselves and begin to resent the other person. Too many people miss this especially important point and marry the wrong person. Maybe there was an initial attraction or common interest, which brought them together in the first place. But a few things in common will not last a lifetime and bring the type of true love I am speaking about.

Let me stop here and mention the pastor of my church and his wife that have been married for forty-two years. He recently wrote an article about ten things they had learned from being married for this extended amount of time. One of the things he mentioned was that opposites attract, attack, but then attach as they become attuned to each other. He goes on to mention how different the two of them were. One of them is outgoing, while the other one is quiet and cautious. He stated the differences brought conflict into their marriage early on, and they had to work through this to bring about a bond that made them stronger.

They learned to give each other space to pursue their own interests, friends and hobbies. They enjoy being together but also enjoy equally their time apart. I will say there are people out there that are looking for someone like this. For some couples, this works for them. I personally enjoy sharing a life with someone that enjoys all the same things I do, and we can share the same interests and hobbies. You must know yourself and what your needs are!

5. *Attraction is important.* There needs to be an attraction between two people that come together in love. When two people often meet the attraction and/or chemistry is what they notice first. It is that magical feeling you have when you are with them that makes you think about them when they are not around. Chemistry is important and satisfying in a relationship. God made us sexual creatures for a reason.

The Bible says it was not good for man to be alone, so God made woman. Chemistry is the spice that fuels the romance in a relationship and keeps it from becoming stale and boring. As we age, our bodies change, but it is always important to keep ourselves as attractive to our mate as we possibly can. I think men and women are both guilty of not doing this as they age and are married for a long time. Regardless of the age we find ourselves in searching for our one true love, this is an important component that cannot be left out.

If you do not have an attraction to someone, they cannot be the right person for you. If it is not there in the beginning, it will not likely come later. God made us as sensual creatures with attractions and desires. When you find your one true love and you can trust your heart to them, it is only natural that you should want to consummate this union in sexual intimacy. Sexual intimacy and pleasure are the glue to holding a relationship together and is where two souls bond together as one. There is a spiritual union of two people so in love they need this closeness with one another. It is meant to be passionate, exciting, and pleasurable.

Too many couples do not keep the spark going, and after several years of marriage, they allow themselves to grow apart in this area and lose attraction to one another. This goes to say you must take care of yourself whether you are in or out of a relationship. You cannot expect someone to be attracted to you if you are not attracted to yourself. This ties back to working on yourself.

True love that stands the test of time and lasts forever needs attraction as this is an important ingredient to keep the passion of love alive. I think of it like two magnets; when they are put together, it is exceedingly difficult to separate them because they just keep pulling in the same direction to be together. Magnets can either attract or repel each other. A permanent magnet is an object that produces a magnetic field around itself. It is this field that enables them to stick to each other. If you have ever been in a relationship and felt this type of chemistry, then you know how wonderful this experience is. If you have not ever experienced this type of chemistry with someone, then you have not found your one true love yet.

6. *Be open to finding someone.* The hardest thing in life is taking a chance. We often fear the relationship will not work out or we will never find anyone. First, let me reiterate if God has given you a desire to find your "one true love," it is because he has someone for you. If you are perfectly happy living your days out being single, then that is what you should do. I have single friends who are incredibly happy being and staying single. They have a circle of friends to socialize with and spend time with and do not want it any other way.

This book is written for those who have searched and waited a good part of their life for their person and believe they exist. I believe they exist as well if that is your desire. In the beginning, God created one man, Adam, and one woman, Eve. He could have created several men and several women and said pick someone, but he did not. We are all created different, but I do believe there is that one special person who is just like you out there waiting for the same, and God can bring this perfect union together. I witnessed this in my own life and knew it was God and not me that brought us together. But the most important aspect is that you must be open and willing to receive what God has for you.

Next, you must put yourself out there in the right places that would allow you to find someone like you. You would not go to a car dealership and look to buy a boat. Car dealerships only sell cars not boats. I have a hard time believing your chances are exceptionally good of finding the right person in the wrong place. I have heard people tell me over the years, "If it is of God, the right person will come up to me in the grocery store." Out of all my single years and all the times I went to the grocery store, *no one* ever came up to me, let alone started a conversation.

I am not saying it could not happen because with God, anything is possible. I am saying it is not likely. My suggestion is to find single adults in your age group that you can get involved with. Find people you have things in common with. This could be a single adult group at a church, single social groups, clubs with your hobbies, etc. Find out what is available in your area that involves single adults. There are good and safe dating websites around, and many people prefer this method for finding someone. Be cautious and smart about online dating because some people are not honest and truthful in presenting who they really are. This even includes Christian dating sites. Most of all, pray and ask God to lead and direct you. If you are following God and seeking His direction, He will lead you to the right person and even confirm it to you.

7. *Know where to start.* I think one of the hardest parts of trying to find your one true love is where to start. Look for someone that shares your same interests. If you have a special hobby or interest, join a group

of people that share that with you. For me personally, I was looking for a Christian man, so I associated myself with single Christian groups. I worked with Christian single groups for several years and made some great friends over the years. You want to place yourself in the right environment to find the person you are looking to be with.

I knew I would not find the person I was looking for in a bar because I did not visit those places on a regular basis. If you know exactly what you are looking for, you can place yourself in that environment and find someone, again, if you do not settle and are willing to wait. In the meantime, enjoy life and make some great new friends along the way!

8. *Have dating guidelines.* Whether you have been out of the dating scene for a while or you are new to dating, I feel we all need guidelines. Dating can be frustrating to say the least! In today's time where some women have become liberated, it is hard to know what the standards are. I will take the view from being a genuine Southern lady and say women like to be treated like a lady. They like to be shown respect and honor, and I will say men and women both need to treat each other with kindness. It can be quite difficult when meeting someone and one person wants to continue to see the other person, but it is not reciprocated.

Often before meeting someone for the first time, it is best to speak on the phone first. It gives you an opportunity to find something out about each other to determine if a meeting is worth the effort. I personally like a gentleman giving the lady his phone number and her calling him. After speaking with each other several times and it is determined the two should meet, I strongly suggest meeting someone for the first time in a very public place and letting someone else know where you will be and with whom. That way, if either person feels it is not going well, they can decide to leave when they want.

At the first meeting, it should be getting to know each other mutually by asking and answering questions of each other. I have found some questions you may ask that tell you something about the other person. They are as follows:

a) If someone wrote you a blank check to go anywhere in the world, where would that be and why? (This tells you something about what they like to do, if they are romantic, fun, playful, etc.)

b) Do you ever see yourself going there? (This tells you if they have dreams and goals with plans to fulfill them.)

c) How and when did your last relationship end? (When someone talks about previous relationships, you can tell if there still is pain, anger or hurt. A person will let you know if they feel they were a victim. Also, you are trying to see if they are in a repeated cycle of bad relationships and choosing the wrong person.)

d) I can tell from your accent, that you are/are not from this area. How did you come to live in this area? (This will tell you something about their past moves and upbringing.)

e) Where do you see yourself in a relationship five years from now? (This will let you know what they are looking for in a relationship. Are they looking just for a companion, a dating partner, a life partner or a commitment that leads to marriage?)

For me personally, if a person I met was not looking for a permanent relationship that led to marriage, I would not date them. I only wanted to date someone that was looking for the same thing I was looking for. A lot of valuable time can be wasted by dating people who are not looking for the same thing you are.

Next, if one person dominates the conversation and only talks about themselves, that is not a good sign. Someone meeting you for the first time should want to know something about you. In a first meeting, you should be able to tell if there is any type of attraction and if you have anything in common or similar interests. Also, for women, they should take note of how they are treated. Does he dress and act like a gentleman? What things does he do that make you feel that way? For men, does the lady act like a lady and dress like a lady, and what things does she do that makes you feel that way?

First impressions are important! Just keep in mind that most individuals will make a good first impression if they are trying. Many times after the first meeting, the guy will say that they will call you. It is after this someone can choose to contact the person again or not. This is not to be taken in a derogatory way if you are not contacted again. It is just a way of finding out upfront whether the match was a good fit or not. Both individuals must feel it is a good fit to proceed to the next step.

It is important when first meeting someone to find out as much as you can about them to determine how much you have in common. This will include their goals in life, spiritual status, political stances, financial stability (as much as you can without speaking with their accountant), family, hobbies, temperament, health (as much as you can without speaking to their physician), and their work.

Another guideline I would like to give about dating is the importance of not having sex with someone right away. When you first meet someone, it is particularly important that you take time to get to know each other. There should be an attraction in the relationship because that is important. As adults, we should exercise self-control.

Growing up in the 1970s, I would often hear young girls say, "It was an accident that I got pregnant." I used to always say to people you either plan to be pregnant or you plan not to be pregnant. There is only two ways. There are too many forms of birth control out in the world not to have unprotected sex. Also, today STDs (sexually transmitted diseases) are at an all-time high. That effects individuals of all ages.

The emotional side involved with sex should be addressed as well. When we engage in sexual intercourse, there is a bond and connection. When the relationship does not work out and this is broken, then once again, we must heal emotionally before moving on. Waiting till you know someone enough to understand if it is going to be a long-term commitment just makes good sense from all sides. Someone who really cares about you and does not want to lose you will be willing to wait for you. I have seen many make this mistake in relationships, and then they must heal from that broken connection before moving on to another one. It makes it much easier to move on when you have not put sex into the combination.

Another guideline I would like to give in dating is to not go backwards. We can never find what is ahead of us if we are looking in the rearview mirror. I have seen too many people go back to previous relationships thinking it would be different this time around only to waste time finding out it was no different. If you feel someone does not have everything you are looking for or need in a relationship, then that is your head and heart telling you get out because it is not the right person for you. We then get out and try to rethink things over and tell ourselves, *Maybe I was too quick to make that decision or maybe I should have tried longer.*

Most of the time, those feelings we have about someone not being right are correct! So learn to listen to your gut level feelings and be strong enough to stand firm in your decision. You will never find your one true love going backwards, and you will waste so much valuable time trying to find the right person when you are with the wrong person. You might even miss them all together if a lot of time is spent with the wrong person. Learn to listen to your feelings and stand up and support those feelings. This makes for a strong person.

9. *Make a commitment.* How long should you date before making a commitment, which leads to marriage? I feel that depends on the age of the individuals involved. For younger singles that have a lifetime ahead of them, they should date for a

longer amount of time. They do not have as much life experience or relationship experience to guide them. Make sure, regardless of your age, you are sure the person you are going to commit to has everything you need in a partner on every level: spiritually, physically, financially. Do they want children? And what are their view on raising children? If they have grown children, what role do they take in the person's life? How do they feel about aging parents and the role they would take? If you both have careers, how will this look? Will they support you and will you support them in the development of each person's career? Do they ask your opinion before making decisions? Are they concerned about your feelings?

So many questions need to be answered before a commitment should be made. Take as much time as needed to make sure all these questions are answered. It was not until I was older and made mistakes in the wrong relationships that I realized the importance of this. Too late to go back and redo those. It is so easy when two people are in love and emotions are high to rush into marriage, but you must stop and examine all the components of a relationship before rushing into marriage or even living together. Life is way too short to waste any part of it trying to figure out how someone can fit into your life. If you are not sure, take more time and just enjoy dating until you can figure it out.

10. *Do not settle.* I think one of the worst things in life is to settle for someone in a relationship that is not what you need or want. I can never stress enough the importance of not settling but waiting for the right person to come along who meets all your

needs. I have a best friend that looks at settling like this.

Look around you. How many people do you think are settling? Probably more than you think. People settle into okay relationships, okay jobs, okay friends, and an okay life. Why? Because life is comfortable. Okay pays the bills and provides a warm bed at night. Some people are fine with okay, and guess what? That is okay.

But okay is not thrilling. It isn't passionate. It's not life changing or unforgettable. Okay is not the reason you risk absolutely everything you have got for the chance that something absolutely amazing could happen.

I have lived my life long enough to see way too many people settle for someone that is not the right fit. I have had family members and friends that were single parents and felt they had to settle for whoever came along because they could not survive on their own financially and emotionally. I fully understand how difficult single parenthood can be. But being with the wrong person can be a living hell or at the least a miserable existence, which is way worse than living life alone. I often tell my single friends there are things much worse than being alone. My hopes are that every person that reads this book takes the time to be honest and ask themselves, *Am I settling or have I settled?* If the answer is yes, what will you do to change this? Life is way too short to be unhappy or miserable.

The other problem I see way too often are individuals that stay in a relationship that is not working and will not work simply because they either do not have the courage to get out or they do not want to be alone. They tell themselves that someone is better than no one in my life. This is not true!

Someone who is not the right fit for you or who is controlling and damaging to who you are is not good for you. It becomes a toxic relationship that poisons you and keeps you from getting out.

Learn to look at relationships with an open mind and not your feelings and emotions. If it is obvious to you that the person you are with is not the right one, be strong enough to get out. Staying in a wrong relationship damages everyone involved and only prolongs the inevitable. I even had a friend of mine tell me that they were keeping the wrong person in their life until they met the right person. They envisioned going into a store one day and running into that right one, and magically, everything would be right. That is a dream world and not reality.

When you are with the wrong person, the right one can never come along. Can you imagine meeting someone and they tell you they are in a relationship with someone just till you came along? I would run away from that person as fast as possible. It tells me that person is not strong enough to stand on their own. I would want a strong person, not a weak one! Be strong enough to know your needs and what you want and to stand on your own two feet alone. That is when you will attract the right person. I have often found in group gatherings people are drawn to the strongest and most confident person. Determine that will be you, and you will find your *true love*!

Patti (in back with purple shirt) with Wellsprings Singles

# CHAPTER 8

―――――― ✌ ――――――

# Guidelines to Keeping Your True Love

Before beginning this chapter, I need to say that the points outlined will not work if you are matched with the wrong person. If the person you are married to is incompatible with you, trying these steps are pointless. It is like attempting to take a square peg and make it fit in a round hole. No matter how many times you try, it just will not work. I state again, if this applies to you, take account of your relationship and decide what you must do. Life is full of choices. Our choices bring good and bad consequences to our life. The decision is ultimately up to you and how badly you want to be in a true loving relationship for the rest of your life.

One indication that you have found your true love is how effortless the relationship becomes. When two people are the right fit, they flow together like a well-oiled machine. Life becomes enjoyable and so easy and effortless. I truly believe with all my heart that is exactly God's design for men and women. In the Garden of Eden, God knew exactly who Adam was and what he needed because God made him. So by taking a rib from Adam and forming Eve, God was able to design the perfect fit for Adam. I also believe it is God's desire for each of us to find that perfect fit with God's direction and help and by following His lead we can!

I can personally say my husband and I have never had an argument. We may not have agreed on everything, but we have never felt the need to argue. We have so many things in common that it leaves very little to disagree on. If something new comes up that we may not agree on, we find a way to talk it out until we come to a mutual agreement. I equally respect his opinion as much as he equally respects mine. The one underlining combination that makes our relationship so special is the overwhelming love we share for each other. People all around us can see that when we are together.

Physical touch is both of our love languages as well as words of affirmation. We are always holding hands, and when we are sitting together, we are touching the hand or arm of the other one. We are genuinely complementing each other and enjoying every moment we are together. I can say that every day I find something new I appreciate and admire about my husband.

Another important part of our relationship is the genuine respect and admiration we have for one another. If you asked me to name all the things I do not like about my husband, I could not come up with one thing. Is this because he is a perfect man? Yes, for me he is. But he is not a perfect human being. The reason I could not come up with anything is because all I see is the good in him. How did that come about? I will tell you. When you constantly focus on the good things in an individual, anything that you may not like fades away. If you focus on all the things that bother you about someone or even dwell on them a lot, eventually that attitude carries over into how you feel about the person. Try focusing on all the good things and see the difference. I promise it works!

My life story has taught me that life can change on a dime and we need to live every day as if it were our last. Make the most of every moment and love the one that fully owns your heart every day. The most important person in your life, besides God, is your mate. Cherish and love them as if there is no tomorrow. Never take them for granted. The following are some simple guidelines to follow:

1. *Love unconditionally.* If you truly love your mate unconditionally, you do not focus on all the things about them you do not like. You can only see the good in them. So many couples I know talk often of the things their spouses do that they do not like and wish they could change. I am here to tell you that we should never be focusing on changing people but loving them right where they are.

   If you are constantly wanting to change something about your spouse, you could be married to the wrong person. I told my husband after we started dating that I loved everything about him and I would not change a thing. He was exactly the man I was looking for. I meant every word, and the same is true today. It so frees him to be all he wants to be with no pressure to be someone else because of me. This is the way life is supposed to be lived. Every day I see things about my husband that are special and compliment him on the good things he does. I take time to thank God for giving my husband to me because I know he is a gift. When you are focused on the good in someone, you have an extremely hard time seeing anything bad. The good will always outshine the negative.

   I have known couples that only feel love or appreciation for their mate when they have done something for them or they do something they like. That is conditional love. I personally do not want someone to love me just because I did something for them. That is love that must be earned. Most people would agree they want to be loved freely for who they are, not who someone wants them to be. I go back to the very definition of true love from 1 Corinthians 13:4–8:

Love is patient, love is kind. It does not envy, it does not boast, it is not proud. It does not dishonor others, it is not self-seeking, it is not easily angered, it keeps no record of wrongs. Love does not delight in evil but rejoices with the truth. It always protects, always trusts, always hopes, always preserves. Love never fails.

Decide today to love your mate unconditionally.
2. *Communication is key.* Take time to talk with each other every day. We live such busy lives that it is hard to find time, but we need to schedule time and stick to it! One of the keys to a successful marriage is good communication. What that means is equal amount of time of talking and listening for both individuals. It could just be about telling each other about your day or sharing things that are on your mind. But spending time talking with each other builds a bond and closeness between two people. It creates a feeling of importance and interest in your thoughts and ideas.

I have talked to couples who have been married for many years, and they have told me that they have nothing to talk about. This could be that they have not practiced the art of communication and need to work on this. It is never too late. My next question would be: Are you willing to listen with real interest in what the other person is talking about? Individuals are enabled with a keen ability to know if someone is really listening with interest versus someone who is not. Practice taking turns talking and have the other person listen and then ask questions about what was said. Look in their eyes and intently listen. If your mate has a hobby or special interest that you are not into, take the time to learn something about what your mate is talking about and interested in. You just might learn something and even like it!

I have talked with people over the years that have been in affairs, and they often tell me the way it started was through conversation. It was because the other person took the time to listen to them and talk with them. That says a lot about our need as humans to communicate with one another. Your mate should be the one you talk with the most, the one you share your deepest thoughts with.

In the modern technology of cell phones, this one thing has hindered our communication the most. Often when I go out to eat, I like to look around to see who is on their cell phone or if they are looking and talking to the person or persons they came with. I am sad to say most of the time people are consumed with their cell phone. I encourage you to limit the time you have your phone out when you are with the person you are in love with. Are they not the most important person to you? If they are, then demonstrate it by making them more important than your phone. Talk to them as if this was the last opportunity you had to speak with them.

Communication in a relationship brings two people closer to together. No matter how long you are together, you will always have the need to sit and talk to each other daily. You may find new things you did not know about your mate. The more you sit and talk, the more important it will become. Some of the best times my husband and I have are just sitting for hours talking to each other. I remember as a child spending hours talking to a friend on the phone. It is the same principle. My husband is my closest friend, and I love spending time talking with him.

As human beings, things are said and done sometimes that are hurtful without really meaning to hurt the person spoken to. If you communicate together well, this can be talked through and resolved. Both people must make communication a priority. Make sure when you are in the dating process that you communicate and develop a pattern of talking things through.

3. *Trust is essential.* Trust in a relationship or marriage is crucial. Lack of trust destroys more relationships than infidelity. No one likes to feel their partner does not trust them. I have seen many marriages end due to lack of trust. I have discovered over the years that individuals with trust issues were often betrayed or hurt by another person which led them not to trust anyone else. This goes back to working on yourself. You must see you have this issue and resolve the problem before entering another relationship. Couples that enter marriage with one person having trust issues have a recipe for heart-

ache and pain. Lack of trust destroys love, romance, and passion.

I know a couple who married and the husband had trust issues. From the beginning of their marriage the husband did not trust his wife to go anywhere without him even though she had never given him a reason not to trust her. If she went to the grocery store, he had to follow her to make sure that is where she went. When she went to work, he would show up at her job to make sure she was actually at work. This became so disruptive that her employer had to get a restraining order to keep him away. The wife was, truly, a prisoner in the marriage because of her husband's issues with mistrust. She tried to get him to go to counseling to work on this and he refused. After many years of living in this terrible marriage, she left him out of desperation to be freed from her prison.

I had a girlfriend that was divorced. Her husband had cheated on her, so that left her with trust issues. She started dating a man and every time she was with him she had to go through his cell phone to look at his text messages and call history. She insisted on having all the passwords to his email and social media accounts so she could check up on him. Needless to say, they did not date very long before the man would not stand for this anymore. I will say that I have never checked my husband's phone or emails and he has never checked mine.

We are fully assured of the love and commitment we have for each other and have no need to verify that.

I strongly urge you not to enter a relationship with someone who has trust issues.

4.  *Have fun time.* You may have heard the phrase, "People who play together stay together." This is true. It is so important to have fun together. If there is something fun you both like to do, make time to do it as often as possible. There are so many memories made in fun times! This is a bonding time in a relationship when you can laugh, cut up, and enjoy life.

    Life is way too serious not to have fun and laugh. Laughter is healthy physically and emotionally. Learn to find things that make you laugh together. I am blessed to have a husband that loves the silly things in life, so he is always finding things to make us laugh. Just recently, we found an old cartoon that was silly and made us laugh. Laughing together brings a closeness in your relationship.

    If you have children or grandchildren, there will be family fun time as well, but I am speaking of the importance of having fun time just you and your mate. I have been on limited income in my life, and still we have found a lot of fun things to do that do not cost. With so many parks and recreation areas and with a little research of the area you live in, there are fun times awaiting you! My husband and I live close to the ocean and love the beach, so we find ourselves enjoying the beach often. We love to dance and have found many dances to go to for very low cost. We love to travel and have had the opportunity to go to some great sites that have built lasting memories for us.

    You and your spouse may have different hobbies or things you like to do in your free time. I encourage you to learn to be interested in their hobby so you can participate with them. If they like to golf and you do not, take golf lessons and learn how. If they like sports and you do not, learn all you can about the sport so you can participate with them. Trust me, they will notice you have taken an interest in what they like and appreciate it, and this will create a deep bond between the two of you.

I have found over my lifetime to never say never to anything I have not given a good try to learn how to do. It has surprised me the things I never liked before that I enjoy now. My husband likes to work in the yard, and he also likes to build and make things with his hands. I have learned how to do those things with him, and we have made a lot of memories from doing those things together.

My husband is a great photographer. In my lifetime, I never had an opportunity to learn much about photography. Since we met and married, I have learned so much about photography, and early in our relationship, I became his biggest cheerleader. His photography is so inspiring that I will not allow him to put anything but his work in our home. Just because your hobbies and interests do not start out the same does not mean you cannot support and enjoy them with each other.

5. *Romance and passion.* This is the spice of life! This part of the relationship will be as good as the commitment on the two people involved. Both individuals must be committed to how important this aspect of the relationship is. It takes effort, consistency, and creativity. The rewards will be a stronger bond in the relationship as well as pleasure in the process.

Romance and passion only happen after the true feeling of love for someone is present. Love is the fuel for romance and passion. You must feel this deep inside your heart to have the strong passion and desire for another person.

Attraction is an important ingredient as well. God wired us that way, so it is important that we always keep ourselves attractive for our mate. After you are with them long enough, you will understand the things they find attractive in you. They will comment on the things they really like, for example, the way you wear your hair, an outfit they like on you, a certain cologne you wear.

Romance and passion use all the five senses: taste, sight, smell, hearing, and feeling. Invest the time in your relationship to make this mutual satisfying for both of you. Find out what your mate's likes and dislikes are in this area. This is only done by good communication and spending the time together. I love to surprise my husband with all different kinds of romance. I do not want our relationship to ever be stale or mundane. A surprise candlelit dinner, a romantic note written and left where they can find it, unexpected flowers or gifts, a new sexy outfit, watching a romantic movie together, a walk along the beach, sitting out under the stars, a ride in the convertible listening to romantic music, dancing slowly to soft music, body massages, sitting together and just enjoying holding hands or kissing, etc. Romance and passion can be created in the simplest of ways because it is a mindset and an attitude that is important.

Keep in mind that men are visual creatures and often respond to visuals as well as touch.

Women respond to atmosphere as well as touch. Both male and female need to feel they are loved and appreciated to feel romance and passion. If this is missing, it is very difficult to feel anything romantic or passionate. It puts out the fire of both! You cannot feel negative towards your spouse and expect to have romance and passion. You have put out the fire before ever building it. Be creative and always look for new ways to add romance and passion in your relationship!

6. *Sexual compatibility.* This is a topic that you hear truly little about. It is a subject not talked about in our churches, and rarely is it brought up or discussed in social settings. Because this is neglected in conversation, it is assumed it is not important in a marriage or relationship. This is not true at all. God made us to be sexual creatures to enjoy, bind us together as one spirit and body and to procreate. If this was such an important part of who we are, then why do we put little importance on it in our relationships?

   I have seen way too many couples over time having sexual relationships less and less the longer they are together and even stopping it completely. The one thing that binds you together repeatedly in body and spirit and brings so much pleasure to you, you want to stop. Why? Could it be because you do not get the enjoyment out of it any more or the newness has worn off? It might even be that it was not that good to begin with and so why keep trying.

   I will admit I believe two people have to be compatible in this area as well as other areas for it to be enjoyable. I had two very dear friends that were both divorced and found themselves single again in their fifties. They were both Christians and dated for over a year before deciding to get married. They did not want to have sex before they got married to honor God, so they waited till they were married. Immediately, after they were married, they found they were not compatible sexually, and no matter how much they worked at making it better, it never was better. Within two years, they were divorced. It was heart breaking for me to see them go through this! Could the answer here be that they should have had sex before they married to find that out? That is something you must answer on your own convictions. I am simply stating that sex is an important ingredient in a loving marriage.

I know there are counselors that help with this and great books written, but I also know there is a compatibility factor. Great sex in a marriage is the bond that helps hold the relationship together because of the intimacy and closeness it brings. Let me also say that there are times in a marriage that one partner may become ill or have a physical limitation that does not allow them to have sexual intercourse. I also know that modern medicine has come out with wonder drugs like Viagra and Cialis to help men with problems in this area. I will share a personal story from a friend of mine that was married over twenty years to her husband. Her husband had a physical illness that left him incapable of having sexual intercourse. Up to this point they had a good sex life in their relationship.

When they were no longer able to have sexual intercourse, she told herself they still can kiss, hold each other, and be intimate in other ways. She found over time that there was less and less intimacy. She confided in me one day as she stated, "Sex in our relationship was the bond that made us close. When that was taken away, I found we slowly drifted apart, and now I feel we are strangers." Sex in your marriage must be mutually satisfying for both parties. If this is not the case, determine to find out why and fix it! Closeness in your relationship depends on this, so make it a priority.

7. *Grow together spiritually.* Always put God first in your relationship and recognize that He brought you together. Pray and read the Bible together and make sure each of your spiritual needs are met. God gave us a spirit and soul for a reason. It is to worship and serve him. As both of you grow spiritually, it will only strengthen the bond between you. My husband and I start and end each day praying together, and we encourage each other throughout the day. We read the Bible and have Bible studies together.

I know my husband will always pray for me, and when life gets tough, that is so reassuring to know you have a spiritual coach in your corner. This is why it is so important to make sure you find someone that is spiritually compatible with you. Your relationship to God is the most important thing in your life, and your spouse must honor and demonstrate that as well. If one partner is jealous and not trusting, then that can damage a relationship and is not of God. We are called to trust one another. If one partner is controlling or dominating, that is not of God. We are called to love and trust freely! God calls us to live freely to serve him and be all we can be. We do not exist for the sole purpose of being what another person wants us to be.

Having been in a previous marriage where I was not spiritually compatible taught me the importance of this and how it can affect children. My former husband saw evil in almost everything including Disney movies, toys and books for children, and even certain holidays. Because of this, my children were deprived of many fun things in their childhood that I deeply regret. Just because an individual claims to be religious or goes to church does not make them a Christian or spiritually compatible with you. Know what and why you believe and make sure you both agree with each other.

8. *Make your marriage a priority.* We live in an extremely fast-paced world with many demands on our time. There will always be things that take our time: work, raising children, household duties, family, etc. You must see the importance of putting your marriage first and making the time to invest in it. Anything rewarding requires time and effort to keep it that way.

I have seen far too many couples choose to spend their time in other ways as a sign that they are not happy in their marriage. I have seen people work extra at their employment to keep them from being at home with their spouse. I have seen people choose to be involved in extracurricular activities or ministry to keep them away from home. I have seen people spend all their free time with their children or grandchildren to keep them from being with their spouse. You must recognize this for what it is: simply a sign of not being happy!

If you want the best marriage possible, you must make it a priority in your life. God's order is he is to come first in our life then our spouse and our children. If you have it out of order, there will not be harmony in your life. My husband demonstrates to me each day that I am a priority to him, and I do the same. I never want a day to go by that he does not know he is loved. Think about this: if our spouse does not make us a priority, who will? We must live and love like there is no tomorrow. No one is guaranteed tomorrow. Life can change at any moment, and when that happens, I want to know I have fully loved and lived my life. I have always wanted to have a testimony of God's love speaking out loud through my marriage. If we really believed that, we would act differently.

We have given marriage a negative impression. If we are to turn this around to create a positive feeling for the next generation, we must create marriages full of love and fulfillment that shine with happiness and joy. Unfortunately, our faces speak volumes of our feelings. I often look at the faces of couples when they are together. If they look unhappy and are never smiling, that tells me a lot. Today when marriage is mentioned many times, a negative feeling of being tied down or having to endure life with the same person is suggested. We must change that imagine.

It is not the design or purpose for two people to be unhappily married. Just like a vintage car neglected can look old, rusty, and unappealing, marriage without love and true fulfillment are not desirable as well. You cannot speak negatively about your spouse and create a good image of marriage to someone that has never been married. Our words convey what our hearts are feeling.

9. *Make a commitment to your mate.* See your mate as the blessing they are to you and show them how much you appreciate them every day. Your true love is a gift to you, and you should always want to show your appreciation for that gift. I know that life does not always turn out the way we plan. I have decided that I will cherish each day, enjoy each moment with my husband, and take each new day as it comes. I will love to the fullest capacity and enjoy caring and doing things for my husband for the pure enjoyment it brings me. I know that as my husband and I age, there will be challenges and limitations that we will face, but I also know that even when that happens, we will enjoy every moment together and love each other every step of the way.

I discovered a perfect example of this type of devotion in two mallard ducks we came across when first moving to Charleston, South Carolina. We rented a small condominium that overlooked the coastal waterway outside of the city. During the warmer months of the year, it was not uncommon to see mallard ducks on the waterway. When the winter months would come, the ducks would fly further south to a warmer climate. There were two ducks that never left the waterway in front of our place. Upon a closer look, it was obvious they were male and female, and the male had a broken wing, which prevented him from flying. Somewhere in his lifetime, he was injured and broke a wing leaving him permanently disabled.

Because mallards mate for life, his female partner would not leave and stayed each winter by his side. She could have chosen to leave each winter and fly to a warmer place where food was more abundant and there was a hotter climate. But she chose to stay beside him and help care for him year-round since he was unable to fly away. She was never far from him and always aware of where he was. She kept him warm in the winter and made sure he had food. It was her commitment and devotion to him that kept him alive. The residents at the condominium made sure they had food in the winter as well and had named them Boo-boo and Marley. These creatures provide a beautiful example of love and devotion! I have included a picture at the end of this chapter of them. They made such an impression on my life story.

Make your mind up now that your love and devotion for your mate is not conditional, but you will love them completely for as long as you both live and be grateful for every second you have. Regardless of what life may bring, you will find a way to show your love to them and how much they mean to you. Everyone can write their own love story. Make the decision today that you will write yours and live it every day. *Because true love is worth the wait! True love is not measured by the amount of time, but the quality of time spent!*

Boo-boo and Marley

Patti and David enjoying life in Charleston

# ABOUT THE AUTHOR

Patti Turner is a graduate of Lee University in Cleveland, Tennessee. After years of serving in full-time ministry working with youth and adults, she became aware of the lack of teaching on how to find the right mate. She is passionate about breaking the cycle of unhappy marriages.

She lives in Charleston, South Carolina, with her husband, David.

CPSIA information can be obtained
at www.ICGtesting.com
Printed in the USA
BVHW020231060522
636247BV00009B/24